SOMEONE
TO LEAN ON

To Jack Isaac Fenton
Born 10 January 1998
This book is my prayer for you
On your journey, may you always find
someone to lean on

SOMEONE
TO LEAN ON

ACCOMPANYING YOUNG PEOPLE ON THE JOURNEY OF FAITH

PAUL FENTON

SCRIPTURE UNION

Scripture Union, 207–209 Queensway, Bletchley, MK2 2EB, England.

© Paul Fenton 1998

First published 1998

ISBN 1 85999 209 9

Scripture quotations are from the New Living Translation of the Bible.

British Library Cataloguing-in-Publication Data
A catalogue record for this book is available from the British Library.

Cover design by Martin Lore.
Printed and bound in Great Britain by Creative Print and Design, (Wales) Ebbw Vale.

CONTENTS

With thanks

To my colleagues at Scripture Union, for their patience in seeing this project to completion – especially to Jo Campbell for drawing out the meaning behind my sometimes clumsy words!

To the many young people, not least Tula, Karl, Anna, David and Laura, who have contributed to this book by allowing me to accompany them on their faith journeys and teaching me so much along 'the Way'.

To Nicki, my wife, for her constant companionship on the journey of marriage we embarked on six years ago. May our road be long, our journey full of wonderful adventures, and may we celebrate in the presence of our Lord when we reach the promised land.

The concept of the revolutionary wheel (in chapter 5) is a combination of various thinking around faith and adolescent development from: J Westerhoff, James Fowler, Freud and other psychologists. But I am closest to the model used by Stephen Jones in his book, *Faith Shaping*, which I find to be the most inspired work in this area. This book is among those listed on page 124.

I have changed the names of the young people mentioned in this book, to assure their privacy.

Kelly's story is not unusual. I first met her on a Christian holiday where, away from home and family, she was able to reflect on the nature of her life and where it was taking her. Considering her background, I think it is fair to wonder why she was so upset. We could put her distress down to the emotion of the moment or an overzealous worship session, or perhaps it was just adolescent insecurities, tiredness or even PMT! However, if we did that, we would be missing the point. Kelly wasn't riding the crest of an emotional wave – she really did feel empty. She had heard the promise that God would be with her, the promise of life in all its fullness. She had followed all the programmes and the rituals. After her initial commitment, she had been on an eight-week discipleship course and become part of the monthly youth service team. She had been baptised and welcomed into membership. And yet she still felt empty. Why? Did she not make a proper commitment the first time and was in need of making one now? Was something wrong in her life preventing her from experiencing God's blessing? Perhaps she had not been filled with the Spirit? Maybe her church wasn't in touch enough with the latest youth trends and fashionable choruses?

As we talked together, Kelly told me how she longed to follow Jesus and know him more intimately. Trying to identify why she felt this way, I asked her what appeared to me a very straightforward question: who did she turn to when she felt low, alone, afraid or confused; when she couldn't understand her feelings, or had questions about who and what to believe? At first she seemed puzzled. Then she thought carefully and answered, 'Well, no one really. I don't know anyone that well to say those kinds of things.' For Kelly, faith had become a lonely existence. Although she was part of a large church and an active youth group, no one had made the time to get to know her personally. No one knew her well enough to identify her need for growth and nurture. No one was close enough to notice something was wrong. No one was helping her move forward on the journey of faith she had begun two years previously. She had no one to ask the thousand questions that circled in her mind, to wrestle with her weighty doubts. She had heard the gospel, made a commitment, signed on the dotted line – and then been left to go it alone. Somehow this didn't seem fair!

When Paul wrote to the young church in Thessalonica, Greece, he spoke of how sharing the gospel was only a part of his love for the people who lived there: 'We loved you so much that we gave you not only God's Good News but our own lives, too' (1 Thess 2:8). Paul was aware that our love for the young in faith must extend beyond a simple gospel presentation. Indeed, he invested years with young churches so that they would grow up to stand fast in their understanding of God's call on their lives and, in turn, support one another. He had written to the church in Thessalonica with some concern: he had been forced to leave them rather abruptly and was afraid they would fail to continue on the journey in Christ he had begun with them. We need to learn from Paul's eagerness to see people not only find faith in Jesus but grow strong in that faith. Paul did not see this as something they should do alone: he knew the value of being accompanied by older and sometimes wiser companions. As a young follower of Christ, he himself had been accompanied by Barnabas as he discovered his own gifting and worked through the trials of a new and growing faith. He knew that when the young in faith stumbled on rocky ground, they would need someone to steady them; when they reached the hilltops, they would need someone to join the celebration; when they faced a crossroads, they would need someone to share in the decision to take the narrow path; when they faced dark valleys of despair, they would need someone to lean on. We too must learn not only to share the gospel of God but our very lives with the young in faith, so that they might never say they have been abandoned to make the journey alone.

This book explores how we as adults young and old, wise and sometimes foolish, strong and often weak, have something very real to offer those who are young in their experience of life. You don't need to run a youth group, get involved in Sunday school, start a rap group or begin a youth service in the crypt of your local church. You don't need to go out on the streets and preach the gospel to the rowdy crowd who hang out drinking into the early hours down the local park. In fact the inspiration for this book comes out of a deep sense of frustration with the traditional approach to youth work and the attitude we have adopted, consciously and unconsciously, towards young people inside and outside the church. In my early years as a youth worker I thought that if we could make church attractive enough, if we could dress it up with all the colours of the rainbow, offer young people exciting programmes, occupy their time with 'youth activities', get them standing up in front of church saying how great God is, have them jump around to the latest wave of music sounds and laser lighting, then they would become committed Christians eager to get closer to God. I was wrong. Some and even all of these things might be helpful in attracting young people to engage with Christianity, but at best they are only a tool for this task. At worst, they distract us from the call to an ongoing journey of faith in Jesus which will lead us to interact realistically with the world we live in, not hide away from it. Perhaps the best approach to take is to accompany others along the journey, young and old alike committing our lives to each other, welcoming new experiences, faithfully treading onwards, following the Way that will eventually lead us to meet Jesus face to face.

Kelly and I talked about how lonely she felt and how lost she was about where to turn next. We discussed some of her many doubts and were able to answer some of her many questions. Where we could not see any answers, we prayed that God would give her the strength to carry them. We concluded by saying it was not right that she should have to carry all these burdens on her own. She did know Jesus, in fact he was and still is very real to her, but no one had ever told Kelly that it was also good to have the benefit of a close companion who could help when her relationship with Christ seemed dry or lacking in direction. We talked about people she knew she could trust, and identified a young woman in her church with whom she might be able to talk about her feelings: someone who would accompany her as she grew older both in years and in faith; someone she could ask questions of; who would open the Bible with her; who would pray with and for her, celebrate her achievements, comfort her when things went wrong and challenge her to stay true to the Way she had chosen. Kelly wanted to move on in her faith but needed someone to share in her life as well as the gospel she had embraced. We prayed together that she would have the courage to go home and put this into practice, and she committed herself to writing to let me know how she progressed. Afterwards a new enthusiasm entered Kelly's contribution to the holiday. She had found a new hope. On her journey of faith in Jesus she would not have to travel alone.

There are thousands of young people who find themselves on their own as they embark on their journey of faith. Perhaps this is why so many of them fail to retain their beliefs beyond their teenage years. Thousands make a commitment to follow Christ in their teens but, when they meet the first real trials of life in the early years of adulthood, they discover that although there were adults willing to share the gospel with them, those willing to share in their lives are few and far between. So they go it alone, and their faith stands still if it stands at all. My hope is that this book will inspire you to set out on the journey of faith with young people and allow them to accompany you in yours. This will not be a theological commentary nor an exhaustive 'how to' on young people. It is written out of the belief that adults have much to offer the young in faith through the formation of natural and expressive relationships. I have been privileged to enjoy many rewarding relation-ships with young people over ten years of youth ministry and I am grateful to those Christians who chose to invest in my life when I was in my early teens. Those faithful Christians chose to befriend me, and some of those rela-tionships have continued to this day.

I hope this book will be a simple but effective tool in encouraging you to open your life to a young person you may already know or are yet to meet. But don't make the mistake of thinking it is all about what *you* can give. Anyone who has invested time with young people knows how much the young in faith have to offer those of us who have been on the journey longer. And as you read, try not to think of it as another idea for youth work and youth out-reach. This isn't really about youth work at all! It is about a way of life, a way I believe Jesus has called us all to start on as soon as we realise it is our responsibility to make disci-ples of all people, short or tall, fat or thin, ugly or attractive, old or young. It just happens that here I focus on the needs of young people which are so evident in our society and especially in the church. In taking up this challenge, we fol-low the example of Jesus himself who loved his friends enough to give them his whole life, even to the point of death, so that we too might know life in all its fullness. And he continues to accompany us when we need him the most.

In return, will we carry forward his message to the next generation? Do we love them enough to share not only the gospel but our lives also? When young people face the joys, trials and challenges of a faith-filled life, will they find that, close by, there is someone to lean on?

A summary in sound bites

- Thousands of young people find themselves very alone as they embark on their journey of faith.

- You don't need to run a youth group or start a rap group to work closely with young people.

- As Paul went about establishing many early Ch churches, he recognised that sharing his life wa integral to sharing the good news of Christ.

- You and I have something valuable to offer young people through who we are.

- As adults, we can offer natural and expressive relationships to young people.

- Just as Christ accompanies us, so we are called to accompany the young in faith.

- Will you make yourself available as someone to lean on?

Chapter 2

THE JOURNEY

To travel hopefully is a better thing than to arrive...
Robert Louis Stevenson, author and poet, 1850–1894

Simon sat on the side of his dad's boat, his feet bathing in the cool lake currents. It was the break of dawn and he stared expectantly at the distant hills, waiting for the sun to lift itself over the horizon. He looked forward to this moment each day. There was something magical about the way the sun crept up, its light chasing away the darkness of the night. As the sun grew stronger and higher, the darkness retreated into the hills where it could hide in the crags, cracks and caves until it was safe to re-emerge when evening came. Every time Simon experienced this moment, even as a young boy, it had touched something deep in his soul. But he had never been able to place that feeling or understand what was so special about it.

His concentration was abruptly disturbed by his brother, Andy, who leapt onto the deck of the boat with a huge roar and chuckle. 'Day dreaming again, brother?' he bellowed.

Simon had to steady himself to stop from falling into the water, then cursed his brother as Andy piled the nets onto the deck for washing. He sang a familiar tune as they pulled at the ropes and strapped away the sails. It was a clear morning and the breeze was light as they worked at cleaning the boat. Andy was particularly bright and breezy this morning, his deep voice singing hearty folk songs despite a long night with no catch. Fishing was their life. Their father was a fisherman, as was his father before them. The two brothers had continued the great tradition and, on the whole, they were good at it, thanks to the faithful coaching they enjoyed at the hands of their father.

The boat rocked gently against the shore as Andy ended his latest rendition. After a short pause, he asked, 'What d'ya reckon to that teacher then?'

'What teacher?'

Andy's face twisted into a grin as he replied, 'You are a dream boy, aren't you?! You know … that teacher everyone's on about … the one John baptised t'other day and said was even greater than he … the one I grabbed you out the pub to meet … he called you "Pete" … Pete! My brother! Pete – the Rock!' Andy chuckled heartily.

Simon shrugged his shoulders. 'I dunno,' he said. 'I've thought a lot about that but I can't make out what he's getting at. Everyone knows I'm no rock. Every time I open my mouth I dig a hole for myself and end up in trouble. People are supposed to be able to depend on rocks to support them, to lean on them. No one ever takes the risk of leaning on…'

Before Simon could finish, his attention was drawn to a large crowd gathering on the shore. As the two brothers watched, a man who looked familiar appeared and walked towards them. As he drew nearer, they recognised him – it was the teacher. 'May I use your boat?' he asked. 'It's just they can't all hear me from here.' The brothers nodded.

Jesus climbed into the boat, sat down and began to teach the crowd. Simon and Andy listened intently.

When he had finished and the crowd was chewing over his words, Jesus turned to Simon and said, 'Why don't you push the boat out further into deep water, and let down your nets for a catch?'

Simon sighed. They had caught nothing all night, and years of fishing had taught him that no fish would be around today. However, he saw a look on the teacher's face and something in it prompted him to obey. The boat was only a hundred yards from the shore when they watched the nets sink into the deep water.

Suddenly Simon leapt up and yelled words I won't record as the nets began to heave. The two brothers pulled with all their might, and Andy roared with laughter as he shouted at another boat to come and help. Eventually they managed to drag on board the biggest haul of fish they had ever seen. Both boats were full to overflowing.

Simon looked across the glittering hoard to Jesus. Wasn't he a carpenter by trade? How did he know where to find these fish? What was he trying to teach them? Why did he choose now to demonstrate his powers? If he could see beyond the deep waters, what else could he see? Could he know and see everything?

As Simon looked into the teacher's eyes, it dawned on him that perhaps Jesus could see into his very soul. All his wrongs and weaknesses overwhelmed him and he fell to his knees. His cry seemed to well out of the very depths: 'Go away, Lord! I am a sinful man!'

Jesus reached out and touched his shoulder. With that touch came a feeling like the one he experienced when watching the sun rise. It was as if a new light were entering his life, chasing away his fears and darkness. His inner turmoil was replaced by a deep sense of peace as Jesus spoke gently to him, 'Don't be afraid.'

As the boats moved slowly and heavily back to shore, Jesus explained to Simon that he would no longer be catching fish but people. It all seemed so bizarre but, in a weird and magical way, it made so much sense.

When they eventually stepped out onto the shingle, Jesus turned to the two brothers. 'Now,' he said, 'leave your nets and follow me.' Andy looked at Simon. They both glanced back at the large catch and the villagers swarming around the boat. Then they followed him.

The journey begins

The Gospels provide us with several accounts of the calling of the first disciples. Perhaps it was something like the story you have just read, which combines what we are told in all four Gospels (Matt 4:18–22; Mark 1:16–18; Luke 5:1–11; John 1:35–42). In responding to Jesus' call, Simon and Andrew embarked on a journey which meant leaving behind all human security. It would change their lives for ever. In Jesus they found someone who would do more than simply walk with them. He would enrich their relationship in God beyond their wildest dreams. They would encounter adventures that took them to new horizons, physically and spiritually. They would touch new heights and experience depths that, had they been on their own, might have been devastating. They would laugh until their bellies ached and cry until their hearts broke. This journey would be like no other. It is a journey we are all invited to take.

I meet thousands of young people who have responded to God's call on their lives and many more who are still try- ing to make sense of it. Many are not unlike Simon – impul- sive, inexperienced, naive, unstable, outspoken, yet ready to 'step out of the boat' and follow Jesus. Like Simon, they may experience the conviction that Jesus can see into the depths of their souls and bring to light all their inadequa- cies, their failures, their vices and desires, their hidden thoughts and greatest fears. Like Simon, they may discover the touch of Christ which brings light to the dark places, healing to the broken-hearted, warmth to the cold-hearted, comfort to the fearful and peace to those in turmoil. They may hear the voice of Christ reminding them that if they follow him they need not be afraid. It is wonderful to see these young people declare they are Christians, called to a new way of living. It is good when the church celebrates that decision with them. However, we must be on our guard that it doesn't stop there. The decision to follow Christ goes far beyond wearing the name 'Christian'!

It is interesting to try and determine at what point the disciples became Christians. Was it when they acknowledged Jesus as the Messiah (eg Luke 9:20)? If so, it was not a very convincing conversion, since they continued to doubt, deny and misunderstand his intentions (particularly in Simon Peter's case, eg Luke 22:54–62)! Was it when they saw him die and rise again (eg John 20:19–20)? But even then they didn't appear to understand the full importance of what was happening, until Jesus came and explained it to them (eg Acts 1:1–8). Was it in their knowing the whole story and experiencing it firsthand? But is knowing and experiencing something enough? Was it when they received the power of the Spirit at Pentecost (Acts 2)?

The truth is, we don't know! We are told that the disciples were first called Christians at Antioch (Acts 11:26), yet this was some time after Pentecost and even after Paul's conversion, eons after Jesus ascended into heaven – rather late for them to know that they were Christians! I prefer what may appear to be a simplistic answer to this question, which is that the disciples became Christians the day they responded to Jesus' call. Naive, inexperienced and uninformed as they were, they chose to follow him and be associated with his name. However, this was just the beginning.

Our use of the word 'Christian' may be unhelpful in attempting to understand who or what we are in relation to God. It is so easily seen as a one-off decision or state of being. More helpful and perhaps more accurate are terms like 'disciple' and 'follower'. One of the earliest descriptions we have of Christians uses the phrase 'followers of the Way', making reference to Jesus' statement, 'I am the way…' (John 14:6). Many churches welcome young people who have responded to God's call at an evangelistic event, or through baptism or confirmation, as if they have 'arrived' or 'graduated' into the Christian club. As if you can purchase a ticket and once you are in, no further work, thought or effort is required – just sit back and watch the show. So often our attitude to the new Christian is like that of launching a new ship: we gather to celebrate the launch, crack open the bottle of bubbly, watch her sail down the ramp and crash into the open sea, then wave her on her way. The journey has begun, but where will she be going and who will help her get there?

A journey of faith

Beginning a journey involves a great deal of faith. For Simon Peter and the other disciples, it meant taking a risk. They did not know where they were going, what to expect along the way or even whether their basic needs would be met. However, they put their faith in the one who had promised to stay with them not only on this journey but to the very end of time itself (Matt 28:20). When we choose to follow Christ, we must do the same. We may not be called so radically to leave behind our homes and work places, but we are certainly called to leave behind our old way of life. Where once we put our faith in individual people or in the securities of this world, Christ demands that we put our faith in him. Having faith does not necessarily mean having security. Some would say that faith in Christ is their security, and this may be so: but faith and security are not necessarily one and the same. Security can paralyse and pacify faith. Faith is a pilgrim journey. Faith means not knowing as well as knowing. I once heard a wise man say that the great enemy of faith is security. If we are secure, we think we can do it all on our own. We don't make room for Jesus and let him work among us. We need to recognise that the journey of faith involves being willing to go beyond what we know into uncharted territory.

It is interesting to observe that Jesus taught the disciples a lesson on faith in a place they should have felt secure – on a lake in a boat, a familiar experience for many of them. A violent storm blew up and the waves were crashing over the boat (Mark 4:35–41). At first they tried, in their own strength, to steer a course to safety, but they panicked and, in their fear, they woke Jesus who had been sleeping calmly in the stern: 'Don't you care if we drown' – as if his sleeping was a sign he could not be bothered to help! With three words Jesus calmed the storm, then he asked them, 'Why are you so afraid? Do you still have no faith?' The disciples had not yet learned that their security could no longer be found in what they knew but, rather, in who they knew.

When we begin our journey of faith in Jesus, he does not promise us calm waters or an even path. We may fear the fierce storm or the dark valley, but we are not alone. Jesus promises to travel with us, and he encourages us to join others along the way. He calls us to be humble as we share the journey together, not trusting in our own abilities but, like Simon, allowing him to shape us as we watch, listen, try, fail, are corrected and empowered by the one who is able to carry us through any storm and lead us through any valley.

A journey together

Zoe handed me a card before she got on the minibus to go home after camp. She had taken the step of faith to follow Christ that week – a painful decision for her as she knew it meant making some difficult changes in her lifestyle. She thanked me for what I had said and waved as the bus began the long journey home. I opened the card and read:

> *Thank you for all you have said and done this week.*
> *Before I came here I felt lost and very alone. I know that*
> *won't all go away now, but I also know I am not alone*
> *on the journey I have begun while I have been here. Jesus*
> *will go with me and I will grow with him and I know*
> *there will be others who will support me on the way.*
> *Please pray for me.*

Zoe had met Jesus for the first time and she knew that this was the beginning of a journey with him. We had celebrated with her, but now she had to go on without our personal help. As I read her card, I prayed that Jesus would provide a significant adult to encourage Zoe, support her and travel with her on the journey she had begun with us. I prayed that she would never find herself 'lost at sea' without someone she could lean on.

The principle of being accompanied on our faith journey is not a new one. Throughout the Bible, God consistently draws one person alongside another to offer support and nurture. We see powerful examples in Moses and Joshua; Ruth and Naomi; Elijah and Elisha; Eli and Samuel; Barnabas and Paul; then Paul and Timothy. Jesus demonstrated this principle himself when he picked out Peter, James and John from among the twelve for special attention. Furthermore, John was said to be 'the disciple Jesus loved' (John 21:20,24). We should not be surprised that all three of them became known as pillars of the church (Gal 2:9). These people journeyed together as God led them and accompanied them. He works through such relationships to strengthen and bless his children and to bring them into a greater understanding of who he is. We will explore this further as we look at the nature of our journeys with young people and how we can share in them together.

Your journey

As we consider how we can accompany others, we are forced to ask where we are on our own journey of faith. Perhaps you 'arrived' or 'graduated' when you became a Christian and since then have become part of a 'club' that has offered little by way of encouragement to continue. Perhaps, as you read this chapter, you recognise that you are alone and going nowhere. I regularly speak with adults who share the same questions, doubts and insecurities as many young people who are grappling with their faith, adults who have been left alone, struggling to make sense of life as a 'follower of the Way'. I hope that, if this is the case, you will recognise the value of responding to the call to take greater risks, to let go of your security, to embrace the unknown as you take a firm grip of Jesus who will lead you to go alongside others as God works through them to speak to you.

We might also ask, 'If I am struggling or just starting out on my journey, what have I got to offer?' Our society demands that we be experts before we can share our knowledge or teach others; it may want to see our qualifications, experience and proof of competence. So we might say, 'If I'm no expert in faith, what use am I in accompanying anyone?' However, God does not operate on society's terms. Paul states that when we are weak we are strong (2 Cor 12:10). Our God finds it far easier to work with us when we acknowledge our dependence on him than when we are confident in our own strength. Jesus chose the foolish and sometimes unreliable Peter to be a pillar of his church, not because of what he already was but because of what he would become as he learnt from an active relationship with the Master himself. God calls all of us to journey with him and with others, whether we consider ourselves novices or sages.

As we go on to explore the nature of our relationships with young people, do consider also the nature of your relationship with God. But do not use it as a stumbling block to prevent you from sharing with others. If you are alone in your journey, then seek out a more experienced Christian to accompany you. A wise Christian will consider it a privilege to welcome someone willing to go with them on their own journey. Meet together and share your fears and doubts. Pray together, listen to each other and consider what emerges carefully. Read the Bible together and learn from what God says through it. Grow in your relationship with each other and you will both grow in your relationship with God. Jesus demonstrated so vividly with the disciples that real spiritual growth takes place primarily in the context of a relationship. This is why we need to develop rich relationships with the young in faith, if we hope to see them grow on their spiritual journey and find their place in the community of believers. I hope that the following chapters of this book will help you. Happy travelling!

A summary in sound bites

- The commitment to follow Christ is the beginning of the journey, not the end.

- Faith is found in the embarkation points in life, not at the arrival points.

- Having faith does not necessarily mean having security.

- Faith means not knowing as well as knowing; faith is the belief in what we cannot always see.

- Security is no longer found in what we know but who we know.

- Our faith grows when we let go of what makes us secure, and follow Jesus.

- Jesus chose twelve men on which to focus his teaching and, within that group, he paid special attention to three.

- Growth takes place primarily in the context of relationships.

- Your relationship with the young in faith will play a fundamental part in the growth of their faith in God.

Chapter 3

TRAVELLING COMPANIONS

Do not walk behind, I may not lead.
Do not walk ahead, I may not follow.
Just walk by my side and be my friend.

As we travelled through Slough in Wayne's clapped-out Vauxhall Nova, we were brought to a halt by a set of red traffic lights. Although I can't remember the subject of conversation as we sat waiting for the lights to turn green, I do remember glancing over my shoulder at the car that pulled up alongside us. It was a top-of-the range car with foreign plates and a left-hand drive. My eyes ran up and down its shiny metallic paint and finely sculptured steel, but it was when I lifted my eyes to look inside that I was surprised by the stare of the man sitting in the passenger seat. As my eyes met his, he smiled and nodded knowingly at me with a curious look. He then turned back to the others in the car with him, pointing at me and nodding again.

A little disturbed by this, I turned back to Wayne and we both shrugged our shoulders, comforted by the knowledge that soon the traffic lights would change and we could leave this strange character behind. Our comfort was soon disturbed, however, by a knock at the window of my passenger door. The man in the car had rolled down his window, stretched his arm across to ours and wanted to speak to me. I cautiously rolled down the window of Wayne's Nova and somewhat hesitantly asked how I could help him. He pointed his finger at me and said, 'I know you!'

I live with a constant fear of meeting people I don't remember, and I found myself stretching my memory to breaking point to think where I had met this man before. What was his name? Where was he from? When had I met him? No matter how hard I tried, I could not find a name or place with which to associate him. So I had to resign myself to the tired old response of 'I'm terribly sorry, I can't remember your name. Where was it we met?' At this point the whole conversation took on a somewhat surreal tone as he responded, 'I've seen you on TV!'

I was just the slightest bit surprised and, for the record, in my recollection I have never appeared on TV. However, I was curious, so I decided to continue this line of questioning to see where it would lead! I asked, 'What programme have you seen me on?' His face lit up, obviously believing that he had indeed seen me on TV and that his suspicions were vindicated. (Wayne's face also showed some surprise as he didn't think I'd ever appeared on TV either!) The man said, 'I've seen you on...'

In that split second, as he began to speak, my imagination ran wild. What could it be that he associated me with? I know, I thought, it'll be something like *Tomorrow's World*, one of those programmes where clever people present inventions that change the destiny of the human race. Perhaps I look intelligent, creative and philosophical!

But then I had to stop myself. I'd be lying if I said that I looked *that* intelligent, and *Tomorrow's World* is not really me. It would be a programme that reflected someone of my size, looks and stature. I know, I bet it's *Baywatch*! You know, those men who run around on beaches, saving the lives of pretty young women, with their red shorts and tanned bodies. It's an easy mistake...

He actually went on to say, 'I've seen you on *Sesame Street*!'

Sesame Street, I thought. *Sesame Street*!

I was lost for any kind of response, but he stuck out his

hand and I instinctively handed him mine. We shook, he smiled, the light changed to green and he drove away!

One group of young people I told this story to said he might just have been trying to say that I look like a muppet! Whoever it was he mistook me for, I know this much: we had a brief encounter, he misunderstood who I was and, as we never had the time or opportunity to take the conversation any further, he will probably live with the belief he has met a TV personality for the rest of his life. He might well be regaling this story to his friends right now. Thankfully, this misinformation won't change his life. But sometimes our brief encounters do lead to mistaken identity and have far more lasting repercussions. We often jump to conclusions far too quickly. Like the strange man in the flash car, we draw assumptions from limited information and then make critical decisions on the basis of those assumptions.

If any of us wants to embark on a journey with a young person, we need to consider carefully the individual we have chosen to travel with and go beyond our first impression of what a young person is like. Is our impression a fair one? Or are we just accepting the stereotypes suggested by television, newspapers, magazines, radio, cynical parents or other adults?

Mistaken identity?

'Young people today...' How would you end this sentence? How do you see young people? It is a good question to ask because it will impact the nature of any relationship you have with them. We all approach relationships with certain assumptions. What are yours? Let's look at what people have said in the past.

As far back as 300 BC Aristotle wrote, 'When I look at the younger generation, I despair of the future of civilisation.' Fifteen hundred years later, a man known as Peter the monk wrote, 'The world is passing through troublesome times. The young people today think of nothing but themselves.

They have no reverence for parents or old age. They are impatient of all restraint. They talk as if they know everything and what passes for wisdom with us is foolishness to them … As for girls, they are immodest and unwomanly in speech, behaviour and dress.'

Does that sound familiar? It strikes me that many of the stereotypes we have of young people today have been associated with the young for thousands of years. If that is true, then why hasn't society degenerated into the chaos we seem to associate with youth. In fact the despair we often display when we refer to young people would appear to be an over-reaction: despite Aristotle's concern and the observations of Peter the monk, many elements of our society have grown arguably more civilised as succeeding generations of the young grew up and made their mark on our world. Bringing things more up to date, if we were to believe half of what is written in the press about young people, the future of our world would be in the hands of a violent, uneducated, sex-obsessed, anarchic and hopeless generation! Is this really the case? Is it possible that we have jumped to conclusions based on misinformation? Maybe if we took more time to go beyond first impressions to scratch beneath the surface and find out what young people are really like, we might come to some very different conclusions.

I often hear the experience of youth – also known as 'adolescence' or 'the teenage experience' – called 'the problem years', when we expect young people to go through a 'stage' of rebellion and to become awkward, stubborn and uncooperative. It is a time when some adults say that they are best left to work it out on their own. Parents find their teenage offspring embarrassing (and young people find their middle-aged parents embarrassing!), and we struggle with how best to handle their moods and constant demands. Schools wrestle with the attempt to educate and control them. The police are occupied with keeping the peace, and with preventing them from abusing alcohol and drugs. I recently attended a consultative meeting run by senior police advisors, which suggested that 'At one time we referred to the drug culture as part of youth culture. Now we are saying that the drug culture *is* youth culture!' Is this true?

All these opinions add up to young people being seen as problematic, difficult and unmanageable. We label adolescence as troublesome because young people appear to be in constant conflict with adults. However, I struggle with these stereotypes which present a negative view of so many young people. We cannot ignore the very real problems some young people face as they struggle to find a place in our post-modern world. However, to brand *all* young people as difficult is a gross generalisation and, I would suggest, a misinterpretation of the facts.

The problem years?

I am often asked by parents what I think is the biggest problem facing young people today. I sense that people want me to say, 'Drugs', 'Sexual promiscuity', 'Peer pressure', 'Failed education' or even 'Family breakdown'. However, to name any one problem would be to blow it out of all proportion. No single issue impacts all young people in the same way. So, what is it that marks youth as so problematic? I believe I can name it in one small but very disturbing word that will instil fear in the most well-balanced adult. It regularly causes splits and heartache in our churches, so much so that many would rather it didn't happen. What is this little word? Quite simply it is 'Change!'

Youth is a time in everyone's life when we have to deal with the most powerful and concentrated form of change we will ever know. Only yesterday Ben was a doting, trustful child. Now he has hit puberty and his world is turned upside-down. Everything he thought was secure has suddenly been unbuckled and let loose. He realises that his parents aren't the perfect people they once seemed: his old man cheats his taxes and his mum drinks too much when she thinks he isn't watching. Church used to be fun but now it's boring and irrelevant. As for the adults in church, they say one thing on a Sunday morning and behave just like everyone else the rest of the week. Everyone is making demands on his time: school wants him to complete his course work; church wants him to join the latest youth project; parents want him to tidy his room and do the washing-up; his mates want him to meet them down the park for some footie. What's he supposed to do?

To make matters worse, his body is out of control. His voice squeaks at the most embarrassing moments. He gets crazy feelings inside for a special person who doesn't even know he exists. His mind wanders and he can't seem to keep it on track. When he wants to sit still, he can't because his body seems to be in constant motion. He feels like he's on a theme park roller-coaster, leaping from one intense feeling to another without knowing how or why. People keep telling him, 'Grow up and act your age', but then say, 'Sit down and do as your told!' By the time he is sixteen, in the eyes of the law he is adult enough to get married, have children and hold down a full-time job; but he's not adult enough to buy a drink in the pub. He can play the lottery and win 8 million pounds (if he's lucky), but some banks won't give him a cash card. If he wanted to, he could join the army and die for his country; but he wouldn't be allowed to vote for it. And people say these are the best years of your life!

During our youth we experience change at breathtaking speed. Almost every day presents us with new experiences from which, in childhood, we were protected by the safety net of loving parents and our own childlike thinking. Many of these changes are brought about by the physical development from child into young adult. We become able to take care of ourselves and are no longer dependent on our parents; but neither are we completely independent. We no longer see things in only simple terms, as we did as a child, but can grapple with complexity (academics call this the change from concrete to abstract thinking). We begin to question things which would never have crossed our minds before, like the reliability of our parents, who we are, who our real friends are and what's the point in God. Our environment changes as we move from a small and homely junior school to the number-crunching and often sterile senior-school system. There we are taught to achieve and succeed, but find that we mostly fail! Eventually we may reach the world of employment, where we exist to earn money and gather possessions.

Considering the changes a young person must adapt to during the early adult years, it is hardly surprising that those watching refer to this period as 'the problem years'.

Underneath the exterior

Is this the nature of youth? Are young people simply a problem? Unfortunately, this is how they are often perceived. However, underneath all the confusion is a real person.

As a fifteen-year-old boy I can remember the response most adults had towards me. I was everyone else's responsibility but theirs. I was no longer a child but not yet allowed to be an adult. People didn't know how to respond to me. I would get on a train with my friends and we would sit next to some adults, who would promptly move to the next carriage because we looked threatening. And we were the youth group from the local Baptist church! People looked at the external and believed what they read in the papers, but never took the time to look beyond the surface. If they did, they would have found a young man desperate for someone to take me under their wing as I came to terms with being a young adult and grappled with adult complexities and responsibilities. If they had asked me, I'd have told them how I felt so alone and unwanted; how I would lie awake at night wondering if I was worth anything to anyone; how I prayed to God that somebody would take notice of me and help me understand what it meant to be a

Christian in a world that wanted me to be everything but a follower of Jesus.

A number of years ago, when I was helping with a 'Life Skills' lesson at a school, I met Carol. She was twelve years old at the time, and this is her account of what it was like to be a young person:

I believe that young people go through a lot of problems. Some go through more than others, some hardly go through any. All these grown-up adults that think they understand us are totally wrong. They are ignorant when it comes to young people. You have to be a young person to understand the emotions we go through.

I think school is FULL of problems along with a few laughs. Year 8 is full right up with problems. I still have one year left before I'm thirteen yet I began to feel these problems a long time ago. Sometimes you feel totally alone in the world, without any true friends or anyone at all that loves you or makes you feel needed. I feel like this all the time and it is as if killing yourself is a good solution to everything and would make everyone happy. But everyone (young people that is) feels like that at least once in their lives, but afterwards they realise it is silly to think like that.

I feel that life is very hard, hurtful and foolish. No one takes people from 10 to 17 seriously. At school they try to have lessons (like life skills) to make young people my age feel understood. But I think it is useless for adults to try doing that because no matter how much they try and think they understand us, they never will. No one sees how sensitive we are or how easily we get hurt which is mostly why they don't understand us.

Carol was very negative about adults and the way so many of us fail to see the person behind the problems. She reminded me that the feelings a young person goes through are real and can be very painful. She quite rightly points out that during our younger years we are very sensitive to what people say and are so easily hurt (and, if the truth be known, that doesn't change for many of us). Carol taught me that when we begin to listen to young people and less to those who use sound bites and negatives to describe them, only then will we really begin to understand them as unique individuals.

Your unique companion

A true friend takes you for who you are rather than for who you pretend to be. There is great security in that kind of friend.

Harry James Cargus, *Encountering Myself* (SPCK), 1978

When we enter into a relationship with a young person, it is best to go with no preconceptions. We may think we know adolescents very well and feel that we have many pearls of wisdom to offer, but this may actually be a hindrance when we encounter individual young people. With knowledge often comes complacency – we think that Experience A plus Experience B means we must have Reaction C. We forget that we are travelling companions and, if we are not careful, we will find ourselves assuming the role of tour guide, relying on our own efforts to help young people find a place in this world and no longer depending on Christ to lead us. While a greater understanding of the nature of 'adolescence' may be useful, it is not essential when we take up the journey of faith with a young person. Carol was right when she said that the harder we try to understand from the outside, the less likely it is that we ever will. A young person soon knows when an adult is trying to fit them into a box. Though it is true to say in general that young people go through a rapidly changing time during adolescence, the response of each individual to that change will be unique. It is not so much a stage they 'all' go through as one where each individual comes to terms with adult feelings and responsibilities in their own time and in their own way.

Understanding adolescence?

If there were one piece of advice I would give to an adult embarking on a relationship with a young person, it would be that you should not see 'adolescence' as a stage between childhood and adult life but, rather, as the very first years of *being* an adult.

When we look at a young person, biology, history and logic tells us that they are no longer a child. Physically, they are able to perform almost any task an adult can do, and in some cases more easily – just look at the young sports heroes who are past it by the age of 21. The medical world tells us that the female body is far better at dealing with pregnancy, and the baby is less likely to suffer from deformities, when the mother is 17, 18 or 19 years old than in later life. In fact, two hundred years ago, people became adults at puberty. It was not uncommon for a woman to be married at 13 or 14. It was only at the end of the last century that the age of consent was raised from 12 to 16. In almost every culture across the world, a woman used to be considered an old maid if she was not married by the age of 20.

Until the last century, most people were considered adults at 12–14 years of age, and society treated them as adults. Within Jewish culture, at the age of 13 for men and 12 for women, the Hebrews passed through the bar mitzvah (men) or the bat mitzvah (women), and attained religious and legal maturity. They could now marry and be responsible for themselves. On this occasion, their father would read from the Torah: 'Blessed is he who has now freed me from the responsibility of this one'.

In our society, we have created the prolonged culture of adolescence. Even though young people pass through puberty at anything up to four years earlier than a hundred years ago (on average, 12.5 years old for girls, compared with 15+ in 1880), even though they are now ready physically and in most cases emotionally for adult life, we withhold adult responsibility from them for up to ten years. We fail to treat young people as adults soon enough, creating a youth ghetto which is being filled by a unique culture of its own and which has only itself as a reference point because adults have removed themselves from the young person's world. We stand on the sidelines and shake our heads at a culture we have created by failing to address a young person's natural progression towards independence, responsibility and relational security. If we are to take young people seriously, we must begin to redress this balance.

If we intend to accompany young people on their faith journey, we must be willing to break the cultural invention of the adolescent years and bring a more accurate understanding to their development as young adults. As children, the young people we are accompanying were dependent on their parents. Now they have reached puberty and their world is rapidly changing. They are adjusting to a new terrain which is no longer straight and narrow: it has peaks and troughs, sharp turns and difficult corners. As young people grow, so does their ability to handle this new terrain, but they are looking for someone to help them understand it, who will treat them with respect, who will be genuine and honest about this journey into greater maturity, who is still growing in their own understanding but willing to accompany them all the same.

As a cultural phenomenon, adolescence has impacted Western society greatly, bringing with it a great deal of conflict and confusion. It is my belief that if we 'adults' stand on the sidelines, shaking our heads and saying, 'Let's hope they grow out of it', then it may be that they grow out of more than we anticipated. They may grow out of all the things we taught them – our values, our beliefs, our faith, our churches. However, if we recognise that at puberty a child is entering the faith-shaping years of early adult life, if we engage with their world and begin to accompany them on the journey they have begun, we may well see God move powerfully in their lives and reinstate their values as equal citizens in the kingdom of God.

Getting involved

It is precisely when a young person is adjusting to adulthood that they need adults who don't simply shout from the sidelines but who will join them as their companions on the journey to greater maturity. Unfortunately, many adults do not want to join. From where we stand it looks a very strange kind of journey. The rules are unclear: sometimes it seems you have to run, sometimes you have to walk, and at times there is no movement at all. Your fellow travellers may seem hostile.

However, when you take the risk and come alongside one of them, you may find that it is not as strange as you first thought. Young people are happy to teach you the rules they know about and help you understand the language they use to get through it. You may discover that their response to encounters along the way is not the same as their peers. At different times each one of them is in a different place: some appear to mature earlier than others, while some seem to stand still for a while and wait for no apparent reason.

You will soon discover that the journey is not unique to young people. Those you meet will share in experiences you can relate to. They are confused when people don't make sense, when they feel let down or when others contradict themselves; you feel that too. They struggle with issues you struggle with; they want to celebrate achievements you long to celebrate. Family, friends, work and play are all as important to them as they are to you. After a while you realise the problems you associated with young people are not that different from your own. No longer are you the adult and they the young person. You are both companions on a much bigger journey that offers tremendous challenges. The opportunity is there ᴛᴏ sʜᴀʀᴇ in them together.

Suddenly it all appears much more exciting and familiar than you had first anticipated. You are still unsure where this will lead or what you might meet on the way, but you know for sure that you have someone you can relate to travelling at your side. Whatever you encounter on this journey, with God's help you can face it together. Whatever our preconceptions or whatever labels we have attached to young people in the past, let's set these aside as we prepare to enter this strange race alongside them. Let's not pretend we are there to lead and they are there to follow; rather, we and they are embarking on an adventure together, travelling companions who one day may even be referred to as friends.

A summary in sound bites

- See the young person beyond the stereotype and the frequently mistaken identity.

- Accept each young person for the unique person that he or she is.

- Learn to appreciate the tension young people feel between what they are able to do and what society allows them to do.

- Youth is better characterised by change than by problems.

- Recognise that you are travelling with a young adult, not a freak caught in a stage between child and adult years.

- Step into their world. You will find it to be more familiar than it first seemed.

Chapter 4

JOINING THE RACE

Let us run with endurance the race that God has set before us. We do this by keeping our eyes on Jesus, on whom our faith depends from start to finish.

Hebrews 12:1–2

As a boy I was one of the fastest sprinters in my school. I looked forward to sports day with great anticipation. The sprint was the highlight of my year. It would be like the all-important derby games in football, like when Arsenal play Tottenham Hotspur. Whoever wins has the privilege of crowing over supporters of the rival team right up to the next game. The losers have nightmares about going to work/school the next day for fear of chants, teasing, practical jokes and generally 'high spirited' behaviour from the opposition. Some chicken out completely and phone in sick; many are so devastated they even display the symptoms! It doesn't matter where your team is in the premier league table by the end of the season – you can bear that – as long as you win the derby game. The annual school sports day was just as significant for me. If I could win the sprint I could hold my head up high, no matter what was thrown at me the rest of the year. I was Number One!

The day would arrive and I'd be a bundle of nerves. The problem was that at junior school you have to endure all the namby-pamby races for the lower years beforehand. This wouldn't have been so bad if they were proper races, but they weren't. Whoever thought up races like the bat-and-ball race? This wasn't a proper race – although I could see some benefit in getting the younger kids to develop their games skills by running up and down, batting a ball in the air without dropping it. But then there was the egg-and-spoon race. Where was the relevance in that? Practice for when you need to rush a boiled egg to your granny down the road at Number 47?! There was the sack race too, a very strange affair. In my opinion legs were made for running, not for climbing into post office sacks and jumping like a crazed rabbit until you fell over!

At last the sprint would come. I would get prepared, pull on my spikes, pin on my number and focus my mind on the task ahead. We would line up, wait for the marker's gun and, on the sound of the shot, we'd run for all our lives worth. This was the real race, and winning it meant everything. As the competitors reached the line, a cheer would go up, the winner broke the tape, the race was won.

On the starting line

Joining young people as they race towards greater maturity may seem strange at first. You may have grown used to doing things a certain way, running your own race, reaching for your own goals: you may even have achieved many of them. Joining this other race may feel as clumsy as stepping inside a postal sack or carrying an egg in a spoon! Most adults feel more comfortable with the familiar, with what is perceived as the 'real' race as opposed to what some regard as the practice ground of youth. But it is important that we take part. And, just like any race, we must think through beforehand what preparations we need to make to have the best chance of winning.

It may feel even stranger because you join not as a competitor but as a running mate. Your companion needs you to stay with them when they run, when they walk, when they feel they can go no further. Sometimes you may need to carry them through a difficult patch; at times they may carry you. You may need to step ahead so that they can follow, or drop behind so that you can push. On occasions you will find them pushing you further than you thought you could go. At all times you are promised the presence of an even greater companion who, though invisible, is willing you both onward, closer and closer to the day he will meet you face to face as you cross the finishing line.

So, as we approach this strange race, where is the starting line? Where do we begin when we have chosen to accompany a young person on the faith journey? With whom should we travel? How do we go about forming the right relationship? What should we take with us? What should we expect to encounter along the way?

Where to begin?

The simple answer to this question is 'where you are'. When we set off on a journey, we can only start from where we find ourselves! So the most likely place to start may well be your local church. Look around at the young people you find there. *Are* there any young people? What activities are they involved in? Talk to youth leaders about what they are doing to encourage their young people to build relationships with supportive adults. Perhaps they could recommend someone who they feel would benefit from positive adult attention. If there are no youth activities in your church, you could begin by making contact with the young people present on a Sunday. Find out who they are and what they do. If there are no young people in your church, you might want to consider your own family. Fewer and fewer young people have godparents these days and it may be that you could offer a positive relationship to a young relative. And what about the children of your friends? Very few people live in complete isolation from young people. It won't take long before you notice just how many there are.

In taking a good look at where you already are, you will probably discover that there are many young people with whom you could build stronger links, but which one is right for you? We can start to discern this by seeking God, asking him to lead us by his Spirit to identify someone he would have us journey with. Having said this, I have rarely found seeking God's guidance easy. I would so like him to speak audibly or to place his finger on a person or situation he wants me to get involved in. It rarely works that way. However, I have found that he leads my convictions. This may appear very subjective, but I believe God excites or moves us about a person or situation to ask the question, 'Does God want me to do something about this?' Sometimes the answer is a firm 'No' and circumstances indicate that we should not get involved. But more often there is something we can do to give support. We must start to seek God and be sensitive to how he leads each one of us to serve him. If you don't sense a firm yes or no, then keep pursuing your instinct, constantly calling on God's wisdom and guidance.

Who to travel with?

What kind of young person should we be seeking? How old should they be? Should they be committed Christians, baptised or confirmed and welcomed into membership, or someone who has not yet vocalised their commitment to Christ? What about those outside the church whose families do not attend? Should it be a young man or woman?

We must be careful at this point not to paint a picture of some ideal. I have already emphasised the importance of not creating false stereotypes. In fact your travelling companion should probably be someone you know already. To you, he has always been little Tommy who you see every Sunday at church – except that Tommy isn't so little anymore and is fast approaching his fourteenth birthday. He was baptised last week, but may still be feeling a little unsure about the faith he has just signed up to. Would he appreciate having someone to help him with any questions or to give support when he finds that his faith and his life clash? Perhaps you need to ask him.

The person we are to accompany may be standing right in front of us. They may not fit the picture we had in mind – but we must keep an open mind. However, it does help to set certain parameters.

AGE?
Age is a very unhelpful guide in understanding the maturity of young people. Many assume that a young person becomes a teenager at thirteen, which may be true in a literal sense but is not helpful when we are referring to physical or psychological development. For some, the adult years may begin as early as seven or eight years old; conversely, for others, it may not start until they are as old as nineteen or twenty. At twelve years old someone we might call a child may be as physically and emotionally mature as a nineteen-year-old. The reverse is also true. Some boys show no signs of maturity until their late teens, while others will be responsible and considerate at eleven or twelve. We must be careful how we use age to define a person and their needs.

A more helpful measurement would be when we observe young people breaking away from the attachment they have to their parents as they move towards greater independence and individual identity. It is at this point that the presence and support of what sociologists call a 'significant other' can be so essential.

CHRISTIAN, OR NOT YET CHRISTIAN?
What should we be looking for as signs that a young person is ready to move forward in their faith? Must we be sure that they are already a Christian? This brings us back to the question of when we know someone is a Christian. Earlier I defined this as being when they decided to follow Jesus.

This does, however, beg another question: when exactly *do* we begin to follow Jesus? When we confess our sins and accept that Christ died for us? When we understand fully what his death and resurrection means? What about the person who knows nothing of the Christian story but who is attracted by the life of a faithful follower of Christ? If Christ lives in and through his followers, can that person be counted as having accepted him? The more we explore this question, the more difficult it is to say exactly when a person becomes a Christian. Maybe it is not our responsibility to judge 'who is in and who is out' but, rather, simply to provide opportunities for all to know and follow Christ. Though it may seem easier to know where people stand when they have had a momentous conversion experience, like Paul's on the road to Damascus, a slow maturing in faith like that of Paul's friend, Timothy, is just as valid.

Taking these things into consideration, we should be willing to accompany anyone who displays an openness to Christ, whether this is seen in their acceptance of who we are or of the gospel we represent. Only when we encounter real hostility should we question whether someone is best left alone. Even then we need to pray that God will bring that person into contact with another Christian who is able to reach out to them. And we should be open to forming relationships with young people both inside and outside the church: Christ's command to make disciples goes beyond the confines of our faith communities.

MALE OR FEMALE?

What about gender? Should a woman only accompany a young woman and a man only accompany a young man? This is a delicate and sensitive area, particularly in view of the great importance placed on child protection within our society. Young people are vulnerable and we must tread wisely. I would suggest that it is safest to keep to same-sex relationships, particularly if the two parties intend to meet together regularly and in places where they need privacy in which to pray, speak freely and read the Bible. Even this is no guarantee that a young person is safe. We need to leave ourselves open to outside scrutiny and to take care that people do not misinterpret our intentions. However, neither should we be dictated to by gossip-mongers.

Having said this, there are issues about which a man would benefit from talking to a woman and a woman would benefit from talking to a man. The opposite sex often brings a helpful perspective that we would otherwise be unaware of. Neither Paul nor Jesus shied away from nurturing, discipling, teaching and bringing women to faith. Equally, we should not be afraid to present to our society healthy and honest relationships between men and women. As this is such a sensitive issue, there are suggestions for secure relationships in Appendix 1.

When to start?

You don't have to wait until your number is called to take your place at the starting line. The race has already begun and you can join it any time you choose. You will always find a running mate and they will almost always welcome your company. They are just waiting for you to step out and join them.

There are, however, some key points, or rites of passage, in the Christian race which offer us clear opportunities to join in. It is at these times that young people are most prepared to accept our company. It is also at these times that, if we neglect our responsibility to accompany them, they are most likely to feel they have been abandoned and give up altogether.

AT INFANT BAPTISM OR DEDICATION

It may seem strange to mention infant baptism in a book about young people, but the journey of faith can begin when a child is quite young. Many of us are asked to be godparents to the offspring of family or friends, but we often fail to make the most of this open invitation to support a child as they mature physically and spiritually into adulthood. When invited to become a godparent, we are being asked to ensure that the child receives the best opportunity to experience God, come to a personal faith in him and, eventually, take their place within the community of believers. An awesome responsibility and not one to be entered into lightly.

A few years ago Nicki, my wife, and I were asked to be godparents to a child from our wider family. We thought carefully about this and decided we had to turn the request down. Neither of us knew the parents very well, the family were some distance away and, with our heavy time commitments, we did not see how we could fulfil the task responsibly. Godparenting involves regular visits and making time to get to know the whole family, not just the child. We did not want to be godparents who were only heard of at birthdays and Christmas. We would want the child to stay with us during holidays, and to babysit when her mum and dad needed space for their own relationship. We would want to encourage her to be welcomed into the local church and, as she grew older, to sponsor her on Christian holidays and events. We would want to hear about her first day at school, and to give support when she competed for school teams or performed in school plays. As she grew into a young adult, we would want to enjoy time with her at her favourite leisure park, and allow her to join us in our activities. We would want to be available when she felt she could not talk to her parents or had difficult decisions to make. We would want to stand with her when she, hopefully, affirmed her own faith through confirmation or baptism. We would want to grow with her on her faith journey, and always make time to meet with her as she gained greater independence in her own life. We would both want to be there for her to lean on when she hit difficulties or unsettled times.

Godparenting is a comprehensive opportunity to share in a person's whole lifetime. Done well, it can be a very significant relationship. We could argue that if all children had responsible and attentive godparents, very few would grow up to find themselves travelling alone on the journey of faith.

ON COMMITMENT TO FOLLOW CHRIST

Many young people make a commitment to follow Christ during their early adult years. For them, it is a time to make key decisions in a number of different areas – school, work, relationships, whether to leave home and when – and faith is no exception. The church will often have its own rituals for celebrating commitment: the new Christians may be invited to share their testimony of how they met Jesus; announcements may be made and after-service lunches laid on, so that church members can meet and greet the newcomers; an Alpha or other Christian basics course may be offered.

Unfortunately, I have seen many churches celebrate when adults come to faith but ignore young people when they make the same commitment. This is a sad reflection of how we unconsciously undervalue the young and fail to take them seriously. If we do not celebrate this occasion, we miss a wonderful opportunity to show how much we value their decision and want to stand with them as they take their first steps in their new faith. If we ignore young people, we should not be surprised when they become frustrated with church and leave.

Whatever we do or don't do to welcome them into church, a young person's decision to follow Christ is an opportunity for us to initiate a relationship with them. Then, when the wider church fails to take notice or provide for their needs, they at least have someone to turn to for support.

AT BAPTISM OR CONFIRMATION

When a young person makes the decision to be baptised or confirmed of their own accord, they will often be excited and on something of 'a spiritual high' as they prepare for the occasion. This is an ideal opportunity for an adult to join in their preparations and to continue to meet with them after the event. Perhaps you could take part in baptism/confirmation classes or help them with anything they don't understand. A young person will often welcome an adult's interest at this time as they enthusiastically take their place within the community of believers.

However, it becomes more difficult to begin such relationships in churches where young people are expected to be baptised or confirmed as a matter of process rather than personal commitment. Many churches place pressure on young people to pass through confirmation or baptism at set ages, when their personal commitment does not meet the significance of the occasion. Where this occurs, it places different demands on those accompanying a young person at a very early stage on their faith journey. It may be wise to counsel such young people to wait if they feel uncomfortable about making a commitment or to help them question why they are agreeing to be baptised or confirmed. It is important that we support them in making up their own minds and that we stand by them, even vocalising their concerns, whatever they decide.

IN DISCIPLESHIP OR CELL GROUPS

More and more churches are running discipleship or cell groups for young people. They are meeting together to discuss what it means to live out their faith in everyday life, to pray for one another, to read the Bible, to praise God and to explore how they can reach out to their peers. These groups provide the context for much needed nurture and pastoral care as well as building young people up to serve God. They also give an opportunity for adults to identify young people who are especially serious about their faith and who would welcome meeting with adult Christians for encouragement and prayer outside the group.

Cell groups or discipleship groups play a role similar to that demonstrated by Jesus so dynamically in his relationship with the twelve disciples. However, these groups should never exist in isolation of the wider church. The disciples continued to worship in the synagogue even while they were with Jesus, and they went on doing so after he left them (eg Acts 14:1). They saw the benefit of meeting with those outside their own small group. They also realised the value of having what some call a mentor or older brother in the faith. Perhaps the clearest example of this in the New Testament is Barnabas who took Paul under his wing (eg Acts 11:22–26); Paul, in turn, did the same with Timothy (eg 1 Tim 1:1–2). I prefer the term 'companion' to 'mentor' as many people misunderstand the mentor/mentoree relationship, seeing it as just an opportunity to teach and correct a younger disciple or to hold them accountable to their faith. These things may well be part of the relationship, but where it is not based on mutual respect and friendship it is at best short-lived and at worst quite destructive.

Discipleship or cell group leaders would be wise to encourage relationships with adults outside the group as part of their strategy. A requirement of such groups is to look carefully at how they integrate into the wider church and, by encouraging relationships with adult mentors or friends, they will have begun to do so. This is yet another opportunity to start a relationship with a young person, which spans their joining and leaving a cell group, and in which both they and the accompanying adult can press on in the much bigger race we are all part of.

IN POSITIONS OF LEADERSHIP AND SERVICE
Some young people will assume positions of leadership within the church as they grow in their enthusiasm to serve

God amongst their local community of believers. We should encourage them to be involved in all our structures within the church, whether this means being on the building management committee, producing the church newsletter, reading the Bible, leading Sunday school or worship, or announcing the notices. If we are really brave, we could ask them to be the speakers in a normal service rather than a specific youth service. (I will develop this in more detail in another chapter as we think about sharing in adventures.)

Any responsibility that involves young people working alongside adults opens the way to forming relationships with them. You can build on the contact you have, inviting them to your home to share a meal with your family or, if you are single, meeting up for a take-away. Over time you can offer to pray or read the Bible with them, and to listen while they talk about how they see life. Those who take on responsibilities such as leading church services or Sunday school may appreciate your advice as to how they are doing and how they could do it better.

All these occasions in church life provide opportunities for adults to draw alongside young people. There may well be other events in the life of your own church which you can use. Keep your eyes open to the possibilities. You will soon find how straightforward it is to set out on the journey of faith together.

How to begin?

OK! So we know where to start, who to start with and when to begin. But *how* exactly should we begin? Do I just walk up and say, 'Hi, I'm Paul and I'd like to accompany you on your journey of faith!'? Errrrr ... No! That might work with a young person who is exceptionally spiritually aware, but will probably frighten the monkeys out of the rest. This journey is a long one; hopefully, you will be in it for some distance to come. So my advice is to begin slowly. Unless you are already working closely with a number of young people, you will probably need to ease into it gently. And it would be wise at this point to let your church leaders know what you are planning. Perhaps they will encourage others to follow your example, or even do it themselves!

Here are some hints about how to begin.

THE FIRST FEW DAYS...

Adopt a natural approach. If you are in church, then chat with a young person casually after a Sunday service. Get to know their name, if they go to school then which one, what year they are in and what it is like. Ask what they are looking forward to during the coming week, or what they are not looking forward to. Talk a little about yourself, what you do and what you are looking forward to. But don't overdo it! A five or ten minute chat is more than enough. Wish them well, go home – and write down what you have talked about. I say this because we easily forget. It is not insincere to jot things down – it is a sign that we are taking someone seriously. During the week, pray for the young person and for what they have shared with you. The next Sunday, seek them out after the service, say hello and ask them how their week went. Be specific by mentioning the things they have already told you – this shows you were paying attention last time. Use their name: this may sound obvious but young people expect adults to forget because we so often take such little interest in them! Enquire about life in general, then go away and do the same as you did the week before.

THE FIRST FEW WEEKS...

After a number of weeks, you may well discover that the young person you are chatting to is beginning to seek you out after church services. Young people soon learn who are the friendly adults they can talk to, and they usually respond positively to genuine interest. When you have reached this point, you can begin to think about the next step. Why not let them know you have been praying for them regularly and that you want to offer support? Perhaps this is the time to invite them to meet your family for Sunday lunch, or you could meet on neutral territory – McDonalds is always a safe bet! Ask about their family, their career hopes, their feelings about church and faith. Ask them what they would like you to pray for. Arrange to meet up again in a couple of weeks' time to see how it's all going.

My wife, Nicki, has strong and positive memories of an assistant from one of her youth clubs who took an interest in what was important to her. He would make the time to watch her compete in school teams and encourage her in her successes. They would meet to play tennis and chat together. He made her feel valuable and drew her closer to the church by taking an interest in the very normal things of life. Our contact and conversation does not always have to be of a spiritual nature; we should also develop ordinary human interests and allow ourselves to enjoy them.

THE FIRST FEW MONTHS...

After a few months your relationship should be fairly well established and growing quite strongly. Your role should be that of a close, but not too chummy, friend. You will be surprised at how quickly a young person will respond to your attention and concern. It may be appropriate now to think about getting together to read the Bible as well as to share what is going on in your lives. Pray openly together and look for opportunities to develop the young person's gifting by connecting them with other adults in the church who may be able to offer them opportunities to contribute to church life. But remember, too, to enjoy each other's company, taking an interest in whatever seems natural to you both. Sometimes it takes many months before we feel comfortable talking about our feelings and our faith with new companions. Work at a pace that is right for you and don't force it.

The process outlined above is just one way you can start from scratch. You may find that you don't need to go through it: young people may simply stumble across your life and be naturally drawn to you, seeing something genuine in you which they are attracted to and which is positive. But however you begin, it should be on the basis of forming a friendship. Paul, Peter, John and Jude all addressed their disciples as friends in the New Testament letters. For that matter, so did Jesus (John 15:15). We too should set out to be friends, drawing alongside with the intention of being 'near' to them. However, the relationship should never become so close that we are unable to direct when required, but never so detached that we are unable to be supportive when needed. To achieve the right balance, we look to the wisdom and sensitivity of Jesus to guide us.

What to take with us?

When embarking on a journey or participating in a race, you are required to take certain equipment with you. What should you prepare to take with you on this journey? Do you need special training or equipment?

More training and further reading is useful but not essential (see Appendix 3 and Appendix 5). The most important thing to take is yourself. Don't worry about what you don't know or don't have: 'Your heavenly Father already knows all your needs, and he will give you all you need from day to day if you live for him and make the kingdom of God your primary concern' (Matt 6:32–33). This race you are about to start involves putting your trust in God alone.

However, God has clearly recognised in the past that we are not very good at trusting in him alone. Thankfully, we have the Bible to guide us and inspire us at all times and in all situations. In it we find God speaking to us of his plans and promises, his gifts and his path, his values and his way. We should make reading his word a priority. If we allow it to permeate our everyday lives, we will be better equipped to face any hurdles we encounter.

Most of all, as we run this race, we should fix our eyes on Jesus to be our prime companion and running mate (Heb 12:2).

A summary in sound bites

- Begin where you are, by being who you are as best as you know how.

- This is not a race where you have to wait to be asked to take your marks. You can start as soon as you have found someone to join with you.

- Don't be afraid to begin with the obvious. Young people who need your company are probably right on your doorstep.

- Join this race as a companion, not as a competitor. You are not in this for what you can win but what you can learn along the way.

- Begin slowly. You are not Linford Christie and this race won't be over in ten seconds.

- At first the race may appear a little strange, but hang on in there.

- Travel light. Leave your agenda behind and be willing to embrace the unknown.

Chapter 5

COMPANY IN A CHANGING WORLD

We are not converted only once in our lives, but many times; and this endless series of large and small conversions, inner revolutions, leads to our transformation in Christ.

Thomas Merton, author, poet and monk, 1915–1968

I was born within the shouts of Highbury football ground, home to the Arsenal, and grew up a proud north Londoner. However, when I was eleven years old my parents decided to move from our home in Islington to a sleepy commuter town in Bedfordshire. At that point in my life London was all I knew: the city had shaped some of my most important years. My friends, my school, our church and, it seemed, my whole life was about to change as we prepared to move away.

I remember quite clearly the day we moved. On an overcast London morning, I made one last walk to the bottom of our street to say a final farewell to a good friend of mine, who was on his way to what was going to be my 'old' school. I didn't really know how to express myself that day; all I could say was 'Goodbye'. That simple word on that dull morning seemed to hold more significance than it ever had before. Inside me I sensed that this was the end of a big chapter in my life and the beginning of an even bigger one. I could almost feel the child in me slipping away as I looked ahead to the adult world I was about to enter.

The change was not an easy one. My sister Janet and I

struggled to adjust to the new way of life in blissful suburbia. Janet had just turned thirteen and she despised our new life. School was a constant battle for her and making new friends wasn't easy. We both longed to be back in London where we felt we belonged. Janet's response to our new world was dramatic and relayed to my parents through rows that broke the sound barrier and threats to leave home. But while she vividly displayed her frustration at being unsettled, I coped by internalising my response. I would occupy my time with play and sport to wear away the lonely hours in alien territory. The quest to be accepted by the 'natives' and make new friends seemed too much like hard work. I found it easier to withdraw inside myself than to endure the desperate search for people who would accept me.

It was at this point in my changing world that my attitude and feelings towards God took on a new dimension. Our family had been trying out churches both in the new town and further afield, but had eventually settled in a reasonably friendly and active Baptist church in the town centre. This was very different to the Anglican church we had lived next door to in London for as long as I could remember, but on the whole they were welcoming. We began to get involved in church activities, and at last Janet found some solace through the activities of the youth fellowship. Unfortunately I was too young to join the youth group and had to wait until I was 'old enough'. The wait was a very lonely one for me.

To occupy my time outside of school and church, I would spend hours out on my bike around the estate. Sometimes I would just go for a walk in the local countryside. These times became quite precious to me, and some of my most powerful memories are of the hours I spent down by the local brook that crossed the back of the estate. A small path ran alongside the river, and you could hide away from the rest of the world amongst the banks, trees and bushes. It was here that, on reflection, I believe I met

God. With no real friends to speak of, I became quite philosophical and found myself turning upwards in pursuit of meaning and purpose in my life. Sometimes I felt so low, I would look at the water and think that ending my life would be better than to keep going without companionship. Those feelings were very real to me at the time. (In reality, drowning myself in the brook would have been some achievement! It was easy to wade from one side to the other and the biggest fish I ever saw was a stickleback!)

It was on those lonely walks that I learnt to talk to God and, given time, God would talk to me. I would ask big questions of him and, though I rarely felt I went away with clear answers, I did gain a sense of peace. I didn't know how to explain or place those feelings and thoughts – even today I still struggle to verbalise what I feel about God: nonetheless, I knew that I felt his presence.

It wasn't until some time later, when I joined the church youth group, that I heard people talk about Jesus and I began to understand his significance. I realised then who it was that had been meeting with me. When people spoke about Jesus, about all he had said and done, I was fascinated. He became my hero and more – he became my friend. I learnt to live with his company whenever people left me feeling alone. Over time I saw myself being transformed by his nature and, though I have not always been as faithful to him as he has to me, I have learnt to see the world through his eyes, finding the purpose and meaning I had been looking for in those early years of change.

A changing world

I have already stated how the world in which young people live is rapidly changing (as it is for all of us). In the midst of this change, we, as significant adults in their lives, can give shape to their experiences. By drawing alongside them, we may be able to bring order out of chaos, sense out of confusion and peace amidst real suffering. Young people are bombarded with change materially, personally and spiritually. But, with the help of a faithful companion, they can begin to adjust to a new way of living.

Reflecting on my own experience, I must conclude that it was more by accident than design that I found purpose in my life. I did not have the benefit of an older companion to help make sense of my changing world. Much of it had to be worked out on my own. That is not to say I am ungrateful to the faithful youth leaders and believers in my local church who taught me and encouraged me, but this was more often by direct instruction and teaching than by nearness and nurture. So often adults are too occupied with planning and executing church programmes to have time to share. But young people have many hidden questions and concerns which will only be discovered by those who make the effort to draw close to them. Sometimes I would be brave enough to go in search of the nurture I needed and knock on a youth leader's door. But even then I'm not sure how much they realised the deeper seeking that was going on inside me.

As a young person grows through the early adult years of peaks, plateaux and troughs, their character is shaped and transformed, sometimes quite slowly and at other times very quickly. During these times there is often a great deal of confusion on all sides: parents struggle to see their offspring take on adult roles; churches struggle to allow young people the space, time and responsibility to assert their feelings, questions and beliefs; schools struggle to meet the needs of each individual and to find the best way for them to fulfil their potential. We so easily forget that it is in the early adult years that so many of our values and beliefs are formed. If we can accompany young people at this time, then we carry forward the greatest message of all. Just as Christ revealed the gospel to those who let him into their lives, so we reveal it to the young people we allow to come close to us. Only then will they see that, through faith in our Lord Jesus, we can make an impact on our lost and darkened world.

PHYSICAL CHANGE

At this time a young person goes through all kinds of physical and psychological change. Being a male of the species, I have to tread carefully when talking about the opposite sex and especially about the physical developments in young women. You would be quite right to question my authority to speak on such a subject! However, having worked closely with young people for ten years, I can say that I have often heard young women talk about the changes taking place in their bodies. The regularity of periods, the growth of breasts and the changing shape of various other parts become regular topics of conversation! Some young women will develop quite quickly, while others will feel left behind. At a time when they feel extremely self-conscious, the wise counsel of a trustworthy adult may be vital to reassure those who feel 'it' will never happen or that they are not big or small enough in the right places. We can affirm them in so many ways: by letting them know that different rates of development are quite normal, asserting their value as individuals, complimenting them on their dress sense and assuring them that we care for them for who they are beyond how they look. Positive words can have a transforming effect on a young person's self-image. You will be surprised at how well they listen and how closely they examine your words.

Young men will need the same sort of encouragement – though machismo may be much in evidence as they assert their sexuality, so don't overdo the compliments! However, they may struggle inwardly with thoughts about the opposite sex which, if you feel confident enough, you can try to address with them. Young men need to learn to see young women beyond the sexual objects presented by our media-saturated society. A wise adult can affirm the value of women and point out the fun and security to be found in positive, platonic relationships. You can also relieve the feelings of guilt that easily build up in a young man's mind by acknowledging that the strong feelings they may have towards the opposite sex are quite normal. We need to get across to them that sexual thoughts are natural and healthy but must be directed and controlled carefully and responsibly. There is opportunity here to look at the very positive things God has to say about sexual relationships in the Bible and, as your relationship with them grows, you might want to look at the various passages together. Whatever you say, try to be positive about sex while acknowledging that we must hold to God's principles and take care.

In addressing physical issues with young people, we help them place their feelings in the context of life as a whole – spiritual, material and physical. We also demonstrate our commitment to them as whole people, not simply their Christian faith.

MATERIAL CHANGE

Along with physical and psychological change comes greater awareness of the world and what is going on in it. Young people are often very socially aware and many band together to support global projects related to injustice, poverty, the environment, animal welfare and the like. In many ways young people put us to shame by their commitment to issues we often pay little attention to in church. The Bible is not short on instruction regarding these very issues, and we would do well to be more involved than we are. In the process, we can show how faith embraces, or should embrace, real global concerns and can have a meaningful effect on the world in which we live. There are Christian organisations at work in these areas, which would welcome financial and prayer support (you will find a list in Appendix 2).

As young people respond to the material world around them, this will naturally throw up questions about their faith. Why do we live in an imperfect world? Why doesn't God do something about suffering? Why does evil so often overcome good? Why do innocent children die? We will look at the struggle with doubts and difficulties in more detail in a later chapter. But, whatever our response, we cannot afford to overlook such questions: they provide key opportunities for us to help a young person come to terms with life and to grow in their thinking.

SPIRITUAL CHANGE

As young people come to understand the way the world works, they must also grapple with the ambiguities every adult believer must adjust to if faith is to grow. Church is no longer the 'play centre' it may once have been. They will begin to notice that Christians display faults that contradict the message conveyed from the pulpit. Your input will be essential as they search for answers as to how to handle situations like the church deacon who has an affair with a work colleague, or the member of the congregation who is caught embezzling. How does God figure in the midst of this? What should the church's response be? I have seen too many young people abandon the journey of faith as a result of frustration with their fellow travellers who appear to live in hypocrisy. We must stand alongside them in this struggle and respond to these issues directly and honestly.

Young people will also need help to understand the spiritual experiences they go through when they begin to sense God's call and touch on their lives. These spiritual experiences may come in a number of ways: through a visiting speaker, a particularly moving service, some verses from the Bible, or when a friend dies; they may come through a youth concert, or a week away at a Christian holiday or festival. God chooses to challenge us in his own time, and whenever he does so it involves change, be it large or small. But we can be confident that he is in the business of changing lives for the better, so we can take the risk of accepting his challenge and be willing to draw alongside young people as they absorb the spiritual transformation they are going through.

REVOLUTIONARY CHANGE

As the young person's world is transformed physically, materially and spiritually, we must help them to acknowledge that these changes are not one-off experiences but part of an ongoing transformation in Christ. They represent a revolutionary process that takes place in all those whose lives embrace our Lord Jesus Christ as his Spirit leads us into all truth. We must keep pressing forward on the journey of faith, allowing ourselves to be constantly transformed by his presence and promise. When Paul wrote to the Christians in Philippi, he put it like this:

> *I don't mean to say that I have already achieved these things or that I have already reached perfection! But I keep working toward that day when I will finally be all that Christ Jesus saved me for and wants me to be. No, dear brothers and sisters, I am still not all I should be, but I am focusing all my energies on this one thing: Forgetting the past and looking forward to what lies ahead, I strain to reach the end of the race...*
>
> Philippians 3:12–14

We serve young people well if we remind them that faith is not a single experience of God but a succession of occasions when God meets with us, we respond to him and we allow him to change us. I have found it helpful to describe this in the broadest sense by using the idea of a revolutionary wheel. Every spoke on the wheel represents a point along the way that Christ has called us to follow, and each spoke is part of the revolution that takes place in our faith experience. Its exact nature may vary from person to person and will depend on individual circumstances and choices. But the wheel serves as an illustration of the ongoing process in which we continually meet with and are changed by God, as we press on towards the finishing line of his race.

Spokes on the revolutionary wheel of faith

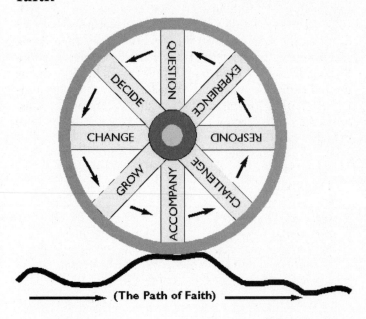

(The Path of Faith)

The 'Accompany' spoke of the wheel is often the first to make contact with the road, since for most the journey of faith begins when a believer chooses to travel with them. As we accompany young people on their journey, we bring them close to an experience of God by allowing them to observe the way we live out our own faith. In doing so, they often begin to shape their world using ours as a reference. This is as much an unconscious process as a conscious one. At times we may consciously encourage them to draw closer to God through

ACCOMPANY

prayer, reading the Bible, or sharing in faith stories and rituals; but it is our constant companionship which provides the picture of faith.

God is accompanying them, too. He has certainly been with me in my life as often as others have been part of it.

As we are accompanied by God, there come times when he chooses to challenge us. The wheel rolls forward to the

CHALLENGE →

'Challenge' spoke. The challenge may come at a meeting or an event; it may come through a person or a book, through a prayer or a conviction. It may be about something we do or don't do, or the kind of person we have become. We will probably meet it with hostility and dislike. It will disturb our thinking and cast us adrift from our

moorings. Anticipating the challenge will be difficult as we cannot predict God's timing, and we certainly cannot force him to challenge others. However, when it does come, it will be something we know we have to respond to.

The wheel rolls forward again. People's reaction to God's challenge will vary: some will fight against it and go

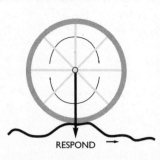

RESPOND →

through a period of struggle. Challenge demands change and this can be painful. We may delay our response for some time and the wheel may remain still, not making any apparent progress. I can recall times in my life when I have struggled to respond to God's challenge for years before relenting. At other times I have accepted the

challenge in a moment! Young people need us to give them time to struggle with their response. The level and speed at which they do may well be a measure of the care we have taken in accompanying them responsibly.

If and when we accept God's challenge, we roll forward to a point where we may experience something of him.

When we say, 'Yes, I accept that you are challenging me, God', we become more open to what he wants to change in us. This experience may come as a feeling or a conviction and, in young people, it may often be quite emotional. A person may receive a vision or a word, and may experience visible release and an excitement difficult to describe. It is something you 'just know' more than you can understand.

Following the experience, we roll forward to a time when we may have many questions. What does all this

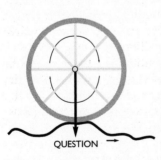

mean? What exactly is God doing with me? How will this affect my life? What should I do about it? Who should I tell? At this point on the journey, a trusted companion is invaluable. They may become a sounding board on which to test out ideas and give shape to any decisions that are made as a result.

As the time of questioning passes and we identify what God is saying to us, then we must make a decision, 'Yes' or 'No'. The wheel rolls forward when we say 'Yes' and comes to a rest when we say 'No'. When a young person says 'No', we should not give up but continue to accompany them: God may well challenge them again, and in time they may respond positively. When a young person says 'Yes', we can

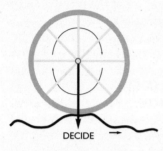

DECIDE →

celebrate with them as they absorb the full implications of their decision and adapt to the change that it brings.

The decision rolls us forward into a time of change. As a young person takes up the challenge and incorporates it into their life, reality begins to hit home. Perhaps they are unable to achieve all the goals they had thought possible. Your company will remind them of the decision they have made and help them remain true to their promises. However, compromise and shortcomings affect us all, and young people will need your support as they adjust to this reality. We cannot become the people God is making us into overnight, or do all that he challenges us to do at once. However, we can press on, allowing the revolutionary wheel to take us to the next stage of the journey.

CHANGE →

As the wheel carries us forward, we grow through the whole experience. The young person matures, as do we, and our relationship with them is strengthened. With each revolution the experience becomes richer. With your help as travelling companion they can gain some understanding of the changing nature of their faith. Most importantly, they will not have been left to struggle on their own.

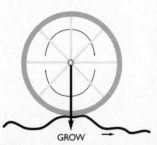

GROW →

And back again to 'Accompany'. The wheel carries us on to more experiences as we accompany one another and

ACCOMPANY →

grow richer through the journey God has called us to. As the process continues, we realise that a revolution is taking place! This is an inner revolution that brings about a wonderful change as we press on towards the end and as God challenges us all over again to draw yet closer to him.

Moses, the changing man

It is interesting to reflect on the lives of people from the Bible and to note how their lives changed as the revolutionary wheel took effect. Moses in particular is a notable example of someone who changed a great deal as God touched his life. In his very early years he receives support from a most unlikely source: one of Pharaoh's daughters is 'moved by God' (Exod 2:6–10) to take the baby Moses into Pharaoh's household. Through her care, and the enlisted help of his real mother, he grows up to be a strong young man. However, he makes a disastrous mistake and is forced to flee (2:11–15). He is left with only God to *accompany* him.

After some time, God *challenges* Moses to go back to Egypt and free his people (ch 3). Moses is forced to *respond* and he struggles with what God is asking him to do. He *experiences* God in the burning bush. He has *questions* about his abilities and finds it hard to believe in himself, so God provides Aaron to be his companion (4:14–16). With the knowledge that he has someone to travel with, Moses *decides* to obey God. He is a *changing* man, gaining in confidence as he *grows* through the various, often dangerous, experiences he encounters along the way. Aaron sticks with him through it all, and so does God, who *challenges* him again and again whenever he falls short of what is required.

The revolutionary wheel rolls forward time and time again in Moses' life. He is a very different man by the time the Israelites enter the Promised Land. He grows closer to God, even being able to speak on God's behalf to the people, displaying God's righteousness and justice, forgiveness and strength (eg Num 12:7–8). Yet there is still the very human side of him that fails him and, as a result, he never enters the Promised Land himself (Deut 32:48–52). But even when he knows this, he continues to run the race, pressing on towards the finishing line.

Changed into his likeness

As the Spirit of the Lord works within us, we become more and more like him and reflect his glory even more.
2 Corinthians 3:18b

The change which takes place within us as we allow God to touch our lives is one that young people will watch carefully. Our every response to the world around us will be weighed and measured as they consider whether or not we are becoming more Christlike ourselves. This can place an incredible burden on us. We may ask, 'What if my faith is standing still? What if I have not experienced an inner revolution in my life for many years? What if I don't display the likeness of Christ?' I can only remind you that your part is not to have arrived on this journey but to join in. Accompanying young people through change will also change you. And there is no more effective way for young people to learn how to cope with experiences of change than for them to witness adults going through the same process. As we allow God to bring about inner revolutions within our own lives, the young people we accompany will recognise that the journey of faith belongs to him, and this may encourage them to be more open to him. However, a problem we face in the church today is that we are resistant to change. As the joke goes – question: how many church members does it take to change a light-bulb? Answer: 'Change? Change? Why does it need to change? What's wrong with it the way it is?!'

The light-bulb needs to be changed because it no longer works. It is broken, and, in many ways, so is the church. Young people are leaving churches in England at a rate of 300 every week (statistic from *Reaching and Keeping Teenagers*, Peter Brierley, Monarch, 1993). Something isn't working and we need to fix it. To fix it properly we must be agents of change, allowing God to do something new while continuing to celebrate the still meaningful rituals of the past. If we want to maintain a strong relationship with the young people we are accompanying, then we must let God, in the power of the Spirit, transform all we are about in the hope that, along with the whole church, we become more and more like Christ, to his ever increasing glory.

A summary in sound bites

- Young people live in a rapidly changing world.

- Be open to change that brings about good.

- God is in the business of changing lives for good.

- Embrace the revolutionary change that God is working out in our lives.

- Learn to recognise what God is doing: accompanying us; challenging us; provoking a response; providing an experience; causing us to question; forcing a decision; changing who we are; enabling us to grow; accompanying us.

- There is no greater way to encourage young people to let God bring revolutionary change to their lives than for them to witness adults going through the same process.

Chapter 6

COMPANY IN NEW EXPERIENCES

I wished for all things that I might enjoy life,
and I was granted life that I might enjoy all things.

Poland had been a big experience – the culture, the people, the climate, the history, the poverty, the food! After seven days of constant activity, thirty-two young people climbed aboard the coach and, with tear-stained faces, waved good-bye to their hosts. The journey home was going to be a long one, approximately thirty hours. We would pass through Poland, Germany, Holland, then France where we would meet the ferry taking us to Dover before we endured a three-hour drive on the motorway.

As the coach settled into the journey, tired limbs began to seek out the most comfortable positions in which to relax and claim back the many lost hours of sleep. I was fortunate to have two front seats to myself, so I stretched out to make the best of them. Just as I felt myself drifting into a longed-for sleep, there was a tap on my shoulder and a quiet voice asked, 'Paul, I'm not feeling too well. Can I sit at the front?' Trying to manage a smile, I climbed out of my seat and allowed Gemma to settle by the window. As I sat down next to her, I realised that the sleep I'd looked forward to wasn't going to happen. Besides, as she was feeling sick, I didn't fancy the idea of what I might awake to!

I hadn't noticed Gemma that much during the week in Poland. She had seemed to possess a fairly composed and amenable character. As we had a long journey ahead, I thought I would find out a little more about her. We chatted about the highlights and lowlights of the past week, what she thought of her exchange family and the places we had visited. We went on to talk about going home and what lay ahead for her there. As the conversation developed, it became apparent that Gemma's family were churchgoers, regularly attending a small and struggling Anglican church near her school. I sensitively enquired about her commitment to the church and the activities she took part in. It transpired that she was the only teenager in the church and was finding it hard to feel any enthusiasm for her part in it. I made a mental note of this and, as the night closed in on us, the quiet murmur of conversation soon went silent as everyone drifted off to sleep.

We awoke as we arrived in Calais for the ferry to Dover, and on board we enjoyed what I can only describe as a blissful English breakfast after a week of potatoes, cabbage and strange looking meat! Back on the coach for the final leg of the journey home, Gemma and I picked up where we had left off. It so happened that she had opted to study religious studies and I would be going into her classes on behalf of Scripture Union to assist with some subjects. I promised that I would catch up with her the next time I was in school and, as we waved goodbye from the car park, she thanked me for listening and for allowing her to sit up front.

Two weeks later, I was in Gemma's religious studies class and stopped behind after the lesson to catch up with her. I asked how she had settled in back at home and if she was still going along to her church. She said she was. Would she be interested, then, in meeting other young people her age who go to church and who get together in the New Year for a Scripture Union residential holiday? She said yes, and I gave her some publicity to read through. Later that year she came along to the New Year holiday and, she tells me, it was there that she made the decision to follow Christ.

Since then Gemma has grown in her faith. She has

worked alongside me during a school work placement, attended leadership training conferences, helped to lead church services, and now often looks after our little baby boy. She has become a real friend to Nicki and me. We meet regularly over coffee for a chat and to pray together. We don't just talk about God either: we talk about boyfriends, college, parents, careers and why the Teletubbies got to Number One! We work through new experiences together and look ahead for new ones to come.

Starting out, moving on

On that school trip to Poland, Gemma and I began a journey together which has seen her meet God in many new ways. It was a new experience for me to accompany Gemma, and I was able to encourage her to venture into a world she hadn't visited before. She was brave enough to go along to a Christian holiday where she would meet a large group of people she didn't know. There have been times when we wrestled over many questions together and she has reached decisions that have taken her forward. Over the past few years Gemma has changed and matured. God has brought about inner revolutions in her life as he has moved her on in her faith journey, and Nicki and I have accompanied her along the way. The journey isn't over yet, and we pray it will roll on for many years to come.

We can see from Gemma's story that a new experience can lead to revolutionary change in someone's life. As we seek to accompany young people on the journey of faith, we should encourage them to take risks and then help them to come through. Such experiences will be remembered as key moments in their life, giving shape to their understanding of God.

Four key areas of experience

In encouraging young people to take risks, we give them creative limits within which to work. Young people often crave adventure and want to try out new things, but our society has allowed a void of meaningful experiences to develop in the key years of young adulthood. And the church is just as guilty of doing the same. Young people are prevented from taking on any real responsibility or encountering valuable experiences until their late teens. Sometimes they are not exposed to anything of significance until their mid twenties. Perhaps this is why we see so many lost in their own culture of drugs, alcohol, material possessions and sexual promiscuity, searching for meaning and purpose. As adults travelling with them on the journey of faith, perhaps we can point them to where they are likely to find real experiences. The following areas may provide such opportunities.

OPPORTUNITIES FOR OUTREACH

This should not to be mistaken for evangelism, although it may involve this. Outreach takes young people out of their homes and cultural norms into areas of need, sometimes in another geographical grouping or place, or in another community or country. It often means entering the unfamiliar, such as travelling to an urban community if you have only been accustomed to a rural one or to a rural community if you have only been accustomed to an urban one. Once there you assist on aid programmes or building projects, perhaps joining with other faith communities as they work out their beliefs in their localities. It is far more enriching to share in the local people's response to their situation than to adopt a 'know it all' approach and try to take over and teach them. The emphasis should rightly be on what we can learn, or what God can teach us, through them. (See Appendix 3 for a list of organisations involved in projects of this kind.)

Outreach can also take place within a young person's own community: we don't need to look far from our own doors to see people in need. If we challenge young people to put their faith into action, we will have achieved a great deal: if we also do it ourselves, we will have achieved even more. Supporting a local soup kitchen for the homeless; visiting homes for elderly people or those with disabilities, physical or mental; chatting with patients at the local hospital: all these things challenge our perceptions and our beliefs. As we open our lives to these new experiences we allow God to speak to us through them, and we may be forced to respond. And so the revolutionary wheel moves on.

OPPORTUNITIES IN THE FAITH COMMUNITY

I use the term 'faith community' rather than 'church' because 'church' has come to have such static connotations and I don't believe church was ever intended to be static. It is more than a building or a service: it is most definitely a community. The challenge is for us to live in a way that makes the church a community. If young people experience it as such, they will have a greater sense of their own part within it. The question is how we can help them to have meaningful and significant experiences within that community. One way we can do this is to discover their potential skills or gifts and see how these can be exercised responsibly.

> *God has given each of us the ability to do certain things well. So if God has given you the ability to prophesy, speak out when you have faith that God is speaking through you. If your gift is that of serving others, serve them well. If you are a teacher, do a good job of teaching. If your gift is to encourage others, do it! If you have money, share it generously. If God has given you leadership ability, take the responsibility seriously. And if you have a gift for showing kindness to others, do it gladly.*

> Romans 12:6–8

When we look within our churches, it would appear as though the 30+ age group has the monopoly on God's gifting. However, the Bible doesn't restrict people's gifts according to age, and young people should be encouraged to take part in the life of the faith community in whatever way seems most natural for them. We must give them the opportunity to exercise their gifts, supporting them when they fail and allowing them space to do so. If there is one place a young person should feel able to fail and find the help to try again, it should be within the church. If only that were more often the case!

We so often compartmentalise youth contributions within our churches, confining them to the youth fellowship or youth service. As good as these occasions might be, they are not integral to the wider faith community. If we want young people to discover meaning in our churches, we must include them in activities that have value to the *whole* church, not just the youth activities. Then they will have experiences they can build on in future years. I was given my first opportunity to preach at the age of fifteen, within my youth group. I have always appreciated it, even though I don't think I was that good at it. But I was encouraged to persevere and the leader's criticism was sensitive. At seventeen, I was invited to get involved in leading a residential holiday. I didn't know anything about it except that I wanted to do it. A local youth worker took me aside and gave me the courage to give it a go. I loved every minute and couldn't wait to come back for more. In ten years I have lead on over fifty residential activities for young people and every time I can't wait to do it again. Through these times my faith has grown tenfold and I have been inspired to keep going on my own journey.

Not all young people will want to lead from the front or preach: they might want to do anything but – however, they may want to help with the PA system, join the music group, do the readings, clean the church hall or sit on the premises committee. Why not find out what they can do and give them an opportunity to belong which they will both value and remember?

OPPORTUNITIES IN FAMILY LIFE
Young people's experience of family will vary enormously. Some will come from stable family units and live with their natural parents, but this in itself will not necessarily mean they have a positive understanding of family. Increasingly we find that young people come from broken families, where they live with only one parent or have step parents or carers. However, a young person's experience of family can be part of the journey towards enriching their understanding of God.

Allowing young people to glimpse the realities of your own family life may well add to their fund of meaningful experiences. Seeing God at work within another family may encourage them to establish good relationships within their own. I remember being allowed to 'sit in' on a family when I was sixteen. I could turn up at any time and they would include me in what they were doing. I'd be given the baby to hold, do the washing-up, help prepare dinner; we would watch television, or sit down and pray together. There were times of frustration and shouting, but there was always love and acceptance. This simple experience was special to me, for it was a family other than my own which allowed me to be part of their lives. I watched and learnt, and I'm sure they have influenced how I 'do' family today.

OPPORTUNITIES FOR PERSONAL ENCOURAGEMENT
As a young person progresses along the journey of faith, you will find that opportunities arise for you to offer more personal encouragement. This can come in all sorts of ways. They may drop hints about things they would like to do or that they feel unsure about. Perhaps they want to further their experience in leadership. Can you encourage them to attend a training holiday or local church course? Maybe you could offer to help finance it?

The simplest of gestures can become memorable. A postcard during exam time, to assure them of your prayers. A phone call after an interview for a college place. A visit when they are unwell. A book to help with difficult questions about their faith. Praying with them when they have fallen in love and are afraid of getting hurt. Reading the Bible with them to reassure them how much God values and loves them even when they feel like the least important person in the world. Sensitively challenging them with biblical truth when they have forgotten what following Jesus means. All these will be meaningful for many young people, and you may be the only adult willing to spend time with them in this way.

Shaping the experience

Encountering creative experiences through outreach, the faith community, family life and personal encouragement brings shape to our understanding of faith and enriches our relationship with God. Our understanding of the world is expanded. We are challenged to explore our faith in more depth. We are presented with choices we must make and consequences we must live with. We have to accept responsibility and risk involvement. We are forced to consider what we should do and how we should do it. We discover new gifts and abilities within ourselves which we never knew were there. Ultimately, we may find that we grow in our understanding of Christ and of how we may be used by him to serve the world around us.

Experiences we will not forget

I have heard it said many times that we remember ten percent of what we hear, forty percent of what we see, seventy percent of what we say and ninety percent of what we do. Our experience of faith is no exception. If young people find themselves without significant memories of faith experiences, come their later years they will find themselves in something of a spiritual vacuum. Faith is grounded in experience; it is realised through *praxis* – putting into practice what we believe and understanding what we believe through what we experience. In the Old Testament, there are many examples of God attaching experience to the instructions or precepts he gives to the people of Israel – the blowing of a horn, wearing particular clothes or acting out particular rituals – all so that they would not forget that he, the Lord, was their God (eg Exod 19:10–13; 28:1–43; Lev 6:14–18). God recognises that very often words are not enough: we seem to need some additional tangible experience before we will really remember them and understand their true meaning. Jesus also seems to have sought to avoid any tendency for his ministry to become static by leaving his disciples with many concrete and memorable experiences on which to build their understanding of God: the healings and miracles they witnessed; the stories he told and the metaphors he used; the simple but powerful imagery of the breaking of bread (eg John 9:1–7; Luke 10:25–37; Mark 14:22–25). As we walk with him along the Way, we too should share more than words and seek to demonstrate faith through actions and images. We must have the courage to risk new experiences with our travelling companions, so that one day they will have the courage to take risks without us.

A summary in sound bites

- Look for the experiences in life that provide new opportunities.

- Take young people beyond their comfortable world to where others live in need.

- Help them to see how the community of believers can be alive and relevant.

- Give young people experiences of family that are real and welcoming.

Chapter 7

COMPANY IN CELEBRATION

*On the appointed day in early spring you must celebrate
… a joyous seven day festival will begin.*

Numbers 28:16–17

There was an air of anticipation. The whole evening had been directed towards this moment. After feasting and drinking, dancing and singing, games and laughter, now the gathered crowd fell silent, waiting. The seconds ticked by. Suddenly the loud chimes of Big Ben leapt from the PA system and filled the room. On the twelfth chime, there was a loud cheer and party poppers burst everywhere. Young people laughed, screamed, shed tears of happiness, hugged each other, shook hands and slapped each other on the back. Happy New Year!

It had been a wonderful celebration. The evening had begun with a banquet. The young people had come dressed in suits, dinner jackets, bow-ties, ball gowns and snazzy dresses. In the finely decorated oak-panelled dining room, with jazz music completing the ambience, they found their seats in small groups of six or eight. After special guests were welcomed and grace was said, the leaders waited on them at their tables. Between each course a veritable feast of entertainment was provided, with comedy, song, poetry and juggling. This was followed by some short speeches before the guests retired to change into more casual clothing and dance another hour away until midnight. Eventually, as the final countdown approached, people

gathered to sing choruses and hymns, to pray, to make res-
olutions and, finally, to wait in silence for the old year to
end and the new one to begin.

Joining the party!

My first experience of this event, which has become known
as 'Countdown', had a remarkable impact on me. Over a
hundred young people and leaders came together for five
days to celebrate and seek God. I had never seen the New
Year in with such passion and joy. I don't know that I had
ever celebrated *anything* in such a way before. My spirits
were lifted and I found a new enthusiasm for the year
ahead. My faith in God reached new heights as I shared in
an experience that has lived with me ever since.

That was ten years ago. Since then I have gone back to
Countdown time and again. Now I am part of the leadership and it remains just as special. Every time we go back I
face new challenges as I celebrate alongside my many spiritual companions who tread the road of faith with me from
year to year. I have seen many lives enriched and changed,
and can testify to the value of having times when we celebrate new beginnings, old promises or recent achievements.

As Christians I believe we have forgotten how to really
celebrate. If we look back to biblical times, we see that celebration was an integral part of everyday life. The people of
Israel often marked important events in their history with
special festivals, indeed they were instructed by God to do
so (eg Deut 16:1–17). These festivals were not sombre, tired
old traditions: they were alive with significance, for example marking God's faithfulness towards them. The rituals
and ceremonies were in equal proportion to the feasting,
drinking, dancing and singing, and in some cases the fes-
tivities lasted not only all night but all week!

They celebrated other, lesser occasions with equal
enthusiasm. We can see from the wedding at Cana how
long and hard people partied, drinking a lot of wine and

quite probably engaging in a lot of dancing and singing too (John 2:1–10)! Almost any excuse seemed good enough to throw a party. In the stories of the lost sheep, coin and lost son (Luke 15), Jesus drew on this enthusiasm for celebration. We should have that same enthusiasm. It is good to celebrate, and it's fun too. We are allowed to enjoy ourselves and to make an occasion of it. One of the fruit of the Spirit is joy!

In my experience, young people love to party. If our faith is going to have any impact on them, then we must be able to celebrate up there with the best of them. Every New Year at Countdown, we party with style and attitude. It's the best party of the year and a memorable experience for all involved. As one young person said to me afterwards, 'I've never had so much fun in all my life.' And why not? I'm sure that's the way God intended it. (See Appendix 4 for a list of organisations that provide holidays like Countdown.)

Knowing when to celebrate

With a little bit of forward thinking we can identify key opportunities to mark occasions that will enrich our relationship with young people and nurture their faith. Below I have identified three areas in which we can celebrate for different reasons. Each area presents a number of possibilities. These are by no means exhaustive and you can probably think of times that are more relevant to the young person you find yourself accompanying.

RELIGIOUS OCCASIONS

Just about all of us celebrate Christmas and Easter. There are other occasions too – Harvest, Lent, Advent, Pentecost. Take a look at your church calendar. However, the more traditional festivals are generally marked by churches, families and youth groups in their own way, and you may not be able to celebrate in a way that is specific to your relationship with the young person you are accompanying.

However, you should make full use of these opportunities to join in with the wider church, and perhaps the two of you can help mark the occasion with more enthusiasm and relevance. Maybe you could introduce new ideas, for example holding a 'last supper' meal at Easter for groups of twelve. Alternatively, at Christmas you could organise a 'travelling' meal to remember the journey Joseph and Mary took to Bethlehem, with guests stopping at the homes of four different church families to eat a different part of the meal. At Harvest you might take a hot meal to someone in need and share it with them. The key is to find ways to celebrate that remain memorable and challenging. These then become occasions for growth as we relate our beliefs to the world around us.

Sometimes it is worth doing something just for you and the young person you are accompanying. You could make something special out of a traditional festival, like watching the sun rise on Easter Sunday morning, using the opportunity to pray and commit yourselves to God all over again. Or you could do something a little out of the ordinary. Very few people I know celebrate saints' days anymore, yet they provide an opportunity for us to remember faithful Christians from the past who have gone before us in the Way. Perhaps you could spend a day or half a day learning about the life and experiences of a particular saint, maybe travelling to a place or church dedicated to them, finding time to pray about what challenges you about this person's life, and then ending the day with a meal or a film.

Religious occasions do not have to be old, tired celebrations with irrelevant rituals and outdated ceremonies. They can be dynamic and inspiring: it depends on what you are willing to put into them.

FAITH BENCHMARKS
Most of us have times in our faith journey which we could tell stories about, times when we have felt close to God or

have been touched, moved or excited by something we have witnessed. Sometimes these are private experiences just between God and ourselves, but other occasions we can share and celebrate with others. It is important that the young in faith hear about your 'faith benchmarks', when God has been close to you or when your understanding of him has been enlarged. The telling of stories remains one of the most compelling means of passing on knowledge and experience, and we are all the more caught up in a story when it is about someone we are close to. We must learn to tell our stories so that young people can identify when God is close to them. We will also be helping them to pass on their faith stories to future generations.

Stories provide opportunities to celebrate too. For example, our own coming to faith for the first time – we may call this our conversion date or day of commitment – provides an ideal chance for us to remember and celebrate what God has done. If yours was a gradual acknowledgement of God (that's OK – you're all the richer for it) and you don't have a specific date for when you came to faith, you can pick any day to celebrate! You could mark this day with the young person you are accompanying by having them round for a meal or going on a trip or a special visit, and then use the opportunity to tell them your story of what happened to you and why. Celebrating an event like this with a young person allows them to get close to your faith and hear how it has changed you. Over time they may want to share their faith stories with you too.

Some faith benchmarks are clear and easily recognisable, for example baptism or confirmation. Our faith communities have written in these benchmarks for us, and remembering them sends a strong message of how important our faith is to us. We celebrate these times like we would celebrate a birthday. Just as a birthday celebrates another year in which we have grown and survived, so our remembrance of our baptism or confirmation celebrates another year along the path of faith. As we mark the occasion we will be able to see, hopefully, that we have not just survived but grown as well.

PERSONAL BENCHMARKS

Our interest in a young person's life is not confined to the obviously faith-centred occasions: we should want to celebrate their personal achievements too. Marking these times can be simple yet so very important and meaningful. The attention you give to these will demonstrate to a young person your genuine interest in them.

What you do will depend on how deeply involved you get in what is happening in their life. It might be sending a card to congratulate them on getting through their first day at a new school, or a small present to mark their finishing their exams; it might be making the effort to turn up at a key sporting event they are involved in, or giving them a call when they have been out on a first date. I have found that young people are much better at doing this for me than I am with them. They love to bring presents, chocolates, cards and messages to mark the occasions they think are important to me. Sometimes there is no obvious reason to celebrate, but we should do so anyway – just to say thanks for being there when it mattered!

Celebrations to be remembered

Many of the celebrations we read about in the Bible help us keep in mind what God has done for us and that his promise to be faithful to us will not end. We need to learn to celebrate God's promises more often and with more style! If young people have powerful memories of sharing and enjoying special occasions with people of faith, then these will most likely be the times that come back to them should they ever drift away from their faith communities. In future years, when their faith may seem little more than a distant event, these memories may well play an important role in bringing them home again. Let the party begin!

A summary in sound bites

- Find a variety of ways to celebrate.
- Celebrate often.
- Celebrate meaningfully.
- Celebrate the little things, what other people forget.
- Celebrate when the young person's faith comes alive.
- Learn to enjoy the party.

Chapter 8

COMPANY IN THE WILDERNESS

We know by doing. Take up thy cross, lift it up yourself on your own shoulder, stagger under it, go on with it, and your intellect will be enriched with what no books could give.

Mark Rutherford, *Last Pages from a Journal*, 1915

Sarah had been working alongside me for two weeks. One day she stopped me: 'Paul, can I ask you something?' I always feel a little nervous when people do that, but I responded, 'Sure. What is it?' She said, 'I feel a little silly asking this, but, well, even though you are a Christian, are there ever any times you wonder if God really exists?'

I had no hesitation in giving her my answer and it's the same today as it was back then – 'Yes!' Yes, there are times when I do doubt God, when I wonder whether all that I believe is real or a figment of my own imagination, when I think about packing it all in and going to work at Sainsbury's (not that there's anything wrong with working at Sainbury's, you understand!). There are times when maintaining my faith seems too hard and God appears so distant.

'Oh, good,' Sarah sighed. 'That's a relief.' She had never addressed her doubts before, and she was beginning to see she wasn't the only one who had them.

Natalie sat in front of me, tears streaming down her face, asking, 'Why me? Why me? Why does it have to happen to me?' During the previous week her dad had suddenly been taken ill. He had been a strong and outgoing man, yet the doctors discovered he had a brain tumour. He was given less than two months to live. It was difficult to find words to comfort Natalie and, when her dad died five weeks later, she had every right to ask why God had allowed this to happen. It took time for her faith to adjust to the realities of her dad's death. For a while I wondered whether it would remain intact at all. Yet she came through this nightmare with a great deal of encouragement from those around her, and now shows great confidence despite her ordeal. However, I know Natalie well and I know that underneath the confidence she still holds tightly to that question, 'Why me?'

Arran stopped me in the corridor and asked if we could have a chat later on in the day. We managed to carve out some time before dinner to get out and go for a walk in the countryside nearby. We both needed the fresh air following all the activities that had been going on at this particular Scripture Union holiday. As we were chatting, Arran asked, 'Paul, how do you know that God is really there?' He had been a Christian for some years, yet he had lost the sense of what it was like to know God and was feeling spiritually dry and alone. We talked about the times when we had felt close to God and when we had felt a long way from knowing him at all. We both recognised that there were times in our lives when God seemed distant and we felt lost without him.

Faith in the wilderness

On a journey of faith there will be times when we find ourselves wandering in the wilderness. These dry periods may come of our own choosing, as we move from one experience to another and take the risk of crossing open ground for a while. Or they may come when we least expect and do not ask for them. Without notice, some circumstance or situation, some feeling or thought throws us into desolation where there is no lush pasture, no refreshing water, no hiding place to be seen in any direction. These wilderness periods will be familiar to any experienced traveller who treads the path of faith. We often find ourselves facing our greatest fears, having to consider who we are and what we really believe all over again.

As they journeyed with Moses to the Promised Land, the people of Israel were forced to spend forty years in the wilderness (Neh 9:16–23). From the moment they set out from Egypt, they had moaned, groaned and complained about how tough it was for them, and had broken the promises they had made to remain faithful to God; so their journey was delayed and many of them died before reaching their new home. Yet it was the wilderness that shaped them as a people and prepared them for what lay ahead. Through it they understood how close God could be to them, and they experienced the extremes of joy and pain. Jesus also spent forty days in the desert where he was tested, tried and wearied (eg Mark 1:12–13). David, Elijah, Moses, Ruth, Isaiah, John – all these people of God have had to spend some part of their lives going through a wilderness experience (Heb 11:32–40). Yet this can be a time of challenge as the revolutionary wheel of faith rolls forward and we are forced to respond to God in some way and to experience him with new depths of understanding. We are changed, for better or worse (James 1:2–4,12).

The young people we accompany will also encounter times in the wilderness. At these times their adult fellow traveller may be the most important person on the road besides them. Our experience may provide a shoulder to lean on when the going seems tough and the road too much to bear. So often the wider church is afraid to address the wilderness experience and pretends it is not there. However, it is a reality we ignore at our peril. A young traveller who is struggling needs someone they can rely on. The thoughts and fears they have at this time may seem too frightening to share with any but the most trustworthy of friends. If they do not have that support during these times, they may stumble and fall, and, like some of the people of Israel who set out from Egypt, they may never reach the Promised Land.

Faith amidst doubt and confusion

Doubts are the messengers of the Living One to the honest … doubt must precede ever deeper assurance; for uncertainties are what we first see when we look into a region hitherto unknown, unexplored, unannexed.

George MacDonald, *An Anthology*, 1946

As a young person adjusts to the adult world, the simple thinking of a child is replaced by the gradual awareness of complexity and the ability to think in abstract terms. God is no longer the magical 'Father Christmas' figure he may once have seemed. If the young person is to adjust to the world around them, they must face questions and apparent contradictions in their beliefs. These may throw their faith into a period of confusion, when for a while it appears that life is not all it was made out to be and some deep soul-searching needs to take place.

Questions come thick and fast and may range from the painfully honest to the wonderfully obscure. Why doesn't God do something when innocent people suffer? Why do so many children die needlessly from diseases and malnutrition? Why doesn't God reveal himself so we know that he is there? If God created everything, who created God? What is heaven like? If God loves everyone, why does he want to destroy people in hell? Why are some born rich and others born poor? Why is my friend crippled by a wasting disease? Why did my dog die? What colour is God? Is God male or female? Is God married? How can we be sure he exists? Why can't I feel God now? How do we know that Christianity is the right religion? Are all other faiths wrong? Why have my parents just divorced? Will I see my Nan in heaven? Why am I here? Is there a purpose to my life? How do I know who I should marry? How do I know you are my friend? What will happen when I die? As adults, we may grow tired of these questions or push them to one side, saying that to believe is enough. We may give well-prepared responses that don't really answer the questions because, quite frankly, we are not always sure what the answers are.

Some people will read through the questions listed above and say that there isn't one they cannot answer. Others will say there isn't one of those questions they have the courage to ask. You yourself may be thinking, 'Yes, why?' Perhaps this is the best approach to take, for at least then we are being honest. I know one church where they had a picture on the door to their youth lounge of a man with a question mark on his T-shirt. The youth leader wanted to create a spirit of openness in that room, where any question or doubt could be honestly expressed and get an honest response. Nobody promised easy answers, but there was a willingness to grapple with the issues. But when that particular youth leader moved away, the new church leader removed the picture and said to the young people, 'True faith does not have any questions or doubts. It has all the answers!' Is that true?

I believe it is essential to go through a time of questioning if we are to mature in our faith. The revolutionary wheel of faith moves forward as we make ourselves open to God's working in our lives. The church is deceiving itself when it tries to protect young people from questions and times of confusion. To hide doubts away or to provide answers they cannot own is at best a mistake and at worst a millstone around their necks which will cause them, in later years, to stumble as they move away from the protection of their home church. We can never remove these questions, we can only delay them being asked, and surely it is better that they are asked within the supportive framework of a faith community than in a world which says, 'Your questions reveal that there is no God.' In tackling these issues we may even find that we have done ourselves a great service too, as many of us may feel that these questions are still unresolved. Together with the young person we are accompanying, we gain the opportunity of discovering greater depths to our faith experience.

What is the role of a fellow traveller on the journey of faith during this time of confusion? I have seen many adults try to adopt the role of the sage, the person with all the answers. Some young people will learn the sage's answers 'off by heart', but this won't help them in years to come when others will challenge those answers and the sage isn't there to back them up. It is much better to explore the questions together and to help the young person arrive at their own conclusions, even if these differ from ours. Should they differ, and we can accept this, then our relationship with the young person is strengthened as we experience diversity yet unity in Christ. 'Doubts precede every deeper assurance', just as a time in the wilderness precedes the journey into the Promised Land.

Faith amidst complexity

It matters whether your faith knows the simplicity on the far side of complexity, rather than becomes satisfied with the simplicity on the near side of complexity.

Our Christian faith is said to be quite simple. You will probably be familiar with the song:

Fix your eyes upon Jesus,
look full on his wonderful face,
and the things of earth will grow strangely dim,
in the light of his glory and grace.

Place your trust in Christ and all will be well. The things that trouble us will seem insignificant compared to the joy of knowing our wonderful Saviour who will always be there to guide us thoughout our lives. Believe and follow, ask and it shall be given, seek and you will find, knock and the door will be opened to you. Is it that simple? It doesn't always seem to work out that way!

On the one hand, I can safely say that my faith in Christ has enriched my life beyond my wildest dreams. On the other, it has forced me to face issues I never dreamed would arise for me. The immediate challenge to us all is to recognise the complexity of our faith, which is not dependent on our feelings of security but in a mystery (Col 2:2–4), one made known to us through the foolishness of the crucifixion (1 Cor 1:18–25). The God of all creation become known to us in human form and died on a wooden cross. This was not the answer the human race was looking for, yet it was God's one final answer to all questions that could ever be asked of him. Will we ever fully understand it?

What is your role as you accompany a young person through such complexity? The greatest witness at such time will not be your words or even your knowledge, although these may help. Your role will be to reveal how you have struggled, and continue to struggle, with such complexities yourself. The very fact that you are willing to grapple with such issues, yet your faith carries on growing as a result, will be a witness to the effectiveness of Christ in your life.

Faith amidst a fallen world

Jesus prayed: 'I'm not asking you to take them out of the world but to keep them safe from the evil one … make them pure and holy by teaching them your words of truth … so they will be in us and the world will believe you sent me.'

John 17:15–21

It isn't easy to play a full part in the world around us, yet remain true to the values and beliefs we have in Jesus. Times of struggling against 'the devices and desires' of modern society may drive many of us, and certainly many young people, into the wilderness. We try to fight against dishonesty and lies, to resist temptation and lust. We struggle with the love of material possessions and resentment towards those who have more than we do. We find it hard to withdraw from gossip and slander, and too easily tear into people with words that hurt and destroy. Remaining 'pure and holy' is a constant battle in the lives of many of us. Western society is increasingly abandoning the broadly Christian values of previous generations, and society's pressure to conform brings conflict and causes friction within faith communities. The tension between the world we must live in and the faith that we hold can become too great a burden for many young people.

The young people we accompany will almost inevitably face the tension between faith and a corrupt world, either consciously or unconsciously. As we journey with them, we have the opportunity to be their eyes and ears, keeping a look out for things they may not notice themselves. The story goes that if you place a frog in a saucepan of water and slowly boil it, it will not notice the change in temperature until it is too late: the frog is cooked alive! (How did someone find this out?!) Young people don't always notice that their values and attitudes are affected by their environment. They may come to us and say they feel dry, alone, distant from God, yet not realise that it is in fact they who have distanced themselves from him through choosing to live a life in conflict with his word of truth.

What is our response? It is easy to judge and criticise, to condemn or to become 'holier than thou'. However, it is far better to help young people confront such realities for themselves. Be honest with them. You will know of times in your own life when you have been scarred by walking away from God, so share these times sensitively, helping them to identify where they may be going wrong for themselves. Offer them choices they can make as a result, not ultimatums. We will all drift away from God at some point in our lives, and these times may leave their mark on our faith experience. However, they also provide opportunities for us to move forward again, to be challenged, to respond, to change.

Some young people will realise that they can be deliberately different from the world around them in a positive way. They can become counter-cultural, choosing to follow or not to follow their peers. Some may choose quite simply not to drink at parties, or opt to save the gift of sex for a future marriage partner. Others may choose to spend their money wisely, give gifts or raise money for charity, or take an active role in community projects. Our response to a corrupt world need not always be a negative one, and we can encourage our fellow travellers to respond before the water boils!

Faith amidst failure

The test of true discipleship is scars and not stars!

I had known Tracy for some time. She was a member of a small group of young people who met each week for prayer and Bible study. At one meeting she appeared to be more distracted than normal. When it was time to make drinks, I asked if Tracy would help and we withdrew to the kitchen. As the kettle was boiling, I remarked that she didn't seem quite herself today. She looked at me as if I'd just dropped a bombshell. Then her face screwed up and she dissolved into tears. I didn't quite know what to do until Katy, another youth leader, came in and at once took Tracy in her arms. The three of us sat down in the dining room and Tracy explained how she'd got drunk last Friday night and had had a one-night stand. She felt terrible – guilty, dirty, used, a failure, rejected by God. This single incident had thrown her from all she thought precious, and she found herself in the wilderness. Thankfully, she was able to share with Katy, who accompanied her through the pain and failure she was feeling. In time Tracy was finally able to forgive herself and allow God to completely forgive her too.

We all face times when we fail and let others or God down, when we are wounded by our own actions. Thankfully, though these wounds may leave scars, with the support of a faithful companion they need not be fatal. It is often through being able to share our feelings of failure with someone we trust that we can experience healing, forgiveness and wholeness. A trusted companion will not condemn – it is not their job to be the one to cast the first stone – but they can pick us up, dust us down and point us in a direction that enables us to progress on our journey of faith. The scars will remain, but they will be marks of our determination to continue to learn, grow, change and be better equipped for future rough times. A true disciple bears many scars, but is assured of God's forgiveness which helps him to persevere along the Way, treading faithfully on with their travelling companion by their side.

When the rubber hits the road

Humanly speaking, I survived mainly because of the efforts and influence of one man: Steve Flashman. Without his friendship, example, guidance, encouragement and all the openings he created for me to put my faith into practice, I would inevitably have got bored and drifted away from the commitment I had made. And I would never have had the opportunities to develop the skills and gifts which I need for my work. When I thought I could do better than him, and failed, he picked me up. He believed in me even when I blew it, and was always ready to give me another opportunity.

Steve Chalke, from the foreword to
Nurturing Young Disciples, by John Buckeridge, 1995

The support of a fellow traveller, a faith companion during the times we spend in the wilderness, may often make the difference between survival and death, spiritually speaking. I cannot overestimate the importance of taking an active interest in a young person's life as they make their way towards God's Promised Land. What is more, you may find that at times it is they who provide you with a shoulder to lean on when you go through the wilderness. However, it is important that, as an accompanying adult, you too have an older or more experienced companion to pick you up, dust you down and point you in the right direction whenever you stumble and lose your way.

Not long ago I remember standing up in front of a group of young people at the end of a week of teaching them from the Bible. That particular session was about working through our wilderness experiences. As I spoke, I admitted that at present I was working through a time when I found myself in the wilderness. I hadn't done anything majorly wrong (as far as I was aware); I hadn't experienced any tragedy; I wasn't wrestling with any questions I hadn't wrestled with before. I just knew that, spiritually, I was finding it hard going. I was having good days and bad days. However, I was seeking God, wanting to know where he was taking me. If nothing else, I knew that the time I was spending in the wilderness was preparation for when I would enter 'a new land' of my own, when I would be better equipped, my faith would have greater depth, and I would be able to serve God more effectively. I told the group that I appreciated their prayers and was glad for the company God was providing for me along the way, for they, the group themselves, were the people that at times I needed to lean on.

Our wilderness experiences may only last for minutes, or they may last for years. But God is always there, and at times our encounters with him in the wilderness have more depth and power than ever before. I am often asked what my Promised Land was like when I finally left the wilderness. I'll let you know when I get there.

A reminder of young people's doubts and thinking:

Chapter 9

WHEN THE ROAD PARTS

There's a kind of release and a kind of torment in every goodbye.

Cecil Day-Lewis, poet, 1904–1972

We packed the last box into the back of the van and gave the flat one last look round before locking the door and handing the keys back to the landlord. We had enjoyed two challenging and fulfilling years in this small town. Now was the time to say goodbye.

Over those two years we had grown close to many young people. It was difficult for a number of them to understand why we were moving away. Two of the lads with whom I had built strong friendships were up early to help pack the van. They also offered their services to move the things into our new home. They sat up front in the cab with the driver as Nicki and I set off ahead of the van in our car. On the way we stopped for a drink and something to eat. As we talked, we reminisced about events and occasions over the previous two years. One of the lads, Liam, I had grown to know very well. I had invested more time in him than any other young person I had been working with. He was fun to be with and keen to learn, and he had grown in his faith. He was one of the young people who was finding it difficult to accept that we had chosen to leave the church and move away. Nicki and I had our regrets too, yet we knew that the time had come to move on. As we arrived at our new home, we sensed the end of one chapter in our lives and the beginning of a new one.

The two lads worked like Trojans, moving boxes and furniture into the house and from one room to another. Later that afternoon we eventually stopped for a drink and some sticky buns. Then it was time to say goodbye. We made all the usual promises to keep in touch, thanked them for their help and walked them to the now empty van. As we said our final farewells, Liam came and gave me a big man hug. Then he broke down and cried. Up to that moment I don't think I realised how close we had grown to each other. I was a little shocked, but I realised that for Liam and for myself this was where the road parted. There would be no more impromptu knocks at the door, no more deep discussions whenever we felt like it, no more late-night videos with overdoses of popcorn and coke, no more crazy all-nighters with the rest of the gang. He would have to find somebody else to be nearby when he needed them. I could no longer be there for him to lean on. I was simply too far away.

Farewell until we meet again

For an adult accompanying a young person on the journey of faith, there will come a time when you will have to say goodbye. This may be due to geographical changes, career changes, relationship changes, or changes in our faith. We as people change, and this alters our relationships with others too. For a time we may be fortunate enough to have relationships where we grow and change together. We learn from one another's experiences and our friendship discovers new depths. At other times, however, the changes are such that it means we must part company with our fellow traveller. The nature of the relationship changes and indeed it is right that it should do so. Relationships which remain static cannot grow or discover the great riches that exist on the road ahead.

It may be difficult for a young person to accept that their older companion has to take a different road. They may feel a sense of abandonment. We need to handle this time sensitively, but we cannot hold on too long. We must have the faith in God to let the other go and trust that our greater companion will watch over them. Of course, this cuts both ways. A young person may find that they must leave behind their older companion, and it may be difficult for the adult to realise that they are no longer needed in the same way. We must prepare for these occasions, whether they are brought about by our own choice or forced upon us by circumstances. When the road parts, we need to consider carefully what we should say and do.

Let us look at some common occasions when the road parts.

GEOGRAPHICAL CHANGES

Perhaps this is the most common reason for relationships to change. People have to move away for one reason or another. It is worthwhile considering this from both perspectives. If it is the adult who is moving away, then I believe we have certain responsibilities to fulfil. We must communicate our departure to our younger companion and involve them in our thinking and reasoning. This will be an important lesson for them, since a time will undoubtedly come when they too must leave the familiar. Their experience of watching you through this time may be key to how well they cope themselves.

We should not make any rash promises we cannot keep: 'I'll call you. I'll write soon. We'll visit in a couple of months. We'll be as close as we've ever been. I promise we won't lose touch'. But we don't always know what the future holds. Very quickly we may think, 'I'll phone tomorrow when I have more time' – and tomorrow never comes; or 'I'll write when I have something interesting to say' – and nothing interesting happens, or if it does it passes so quickly, by the time we remember it's old news. These are the realities of change. We find new friends, new travelling companions and they will grow to mean as much to us as our previous companions did. If you are going to promise to write, then make sure you stick to your promise. If you want to invite the young person to visit, then set a date before you go.

Perhaps the most important piece of advice you can give them is that they find a new adult to accompany them when you have gone. There are times when we need to be released from relationships by those we are involved with. If an older companion leaves without providing this release, then the young person may feel that they are betraying their former friend when they begin to confide in someone new. We should encourage them to seek out a new companion and commend them when they tell us they have done so. Make it clear that you will continue to be available and will always be pleased to hear from them. But distance will, by its very nature, change your relationship. Ultimately, we must let them walk on without us and pray that God will provide them with someone new to lean on.

When it is the young person who is moving away, the accompanying adult will still have a responsibility. Once again we must be careful about making promises and creating unrealistic expectations. It will be important to maintain contact if the young person is settling into a new home, school, job or university. You may be the anchor they need as they move from familiar surroundings to unfamiliar ones. Do visit if you can, or invite them to visit you, and share the stories of what is happening in your respective lives. Sometimes this is not possible, and impromptu phone calls or short postcards will be enough. Once again, you must urge them to seek a new travelling companion. Continue to pray for them, and remind them from time to time, via the phone or a postcard, of their 'faith benchmarks' so that they can see where they have been and look forward to where the journey of faith may lead them in the future. But again, don't hold on too tightly. Allow God to move you both on, no matter how difficult this may seem.

CAREER CHANGES

A new job, or a change in the pattern of our working life, may have an impact on the nature of our relationships. Again, it is the accompanying adult who must take the lead in directing the relationship rather than let it just drift apart. You may have less free time or be busier than you were. You may no longer be able to meet as often or as informally as you once did. The first step is to recognise that since your time commitment has changed, your relationship will change too. This may simply mean that you will have to structure your time together more carefully. Find a way to meet that is fun for you both. This may be once a week for Sunday lunch, or once a month for a round of golf! These should be occasions you look forward to, for swapping stories, praying together and seeking God.

Amidst a busy career or a busy time schedule, we must be disciplined about setting aside enough time to spend with the young person we are accompanying and with God, so that together we can continue to move forward on the journey of faith.

RELATIONSHIP CHANGES

As young people grow older, their relationship networks will grow too. There will be more people to share with; more adults willing to talk with them about life, faith and future ambitions; more people to take up their time. There may even come a time when they meet the person they choose to marry. All these relationships will have an impact on the journey you are sharing together. It is important to constantly review whether it is time to allow your younger companion to travel on with a new friend or partner. If it is, then we must give them the freedom to do so and encourage them in their new walk. It is better to recognise that you

have finished your part of this journey and it is now someone else's turn to accompany them from this point on.

However, again, this may not have to mean the end of
your companionship, only a change in its nature. As with a
change in career, you may need to be more structured and
purposeful with the time you spend together. Perhaps your
companion needs to meet with you simply to pray and read
the Bible. Others may fill the roles you once had, but you
can still offer support in a specific area of their life. It is very
rare that we walk the path of faith with just one person: at
times we will share the journey with many different travellers, each one bringing something of value and importance to our faith experience. We must recognise this as it
happens and be willing to change our relationship to meet
whatever need is evident.

FAITH CHANGES

This may be the most challenging change we go through as
we accompany a young person on the journey of faith. As
their faith grows and changes, as God challenges them and
they experience him in new depth, as the revolutionary
wheel of faith rolls forward, a time may come when they
will look for someone else to be alongside them for a while.
Their faith may have grown to a point where it might be
better that they were with someone who can develop their
gifting and give them advice that better fits their need. They
may have outgrown us!

We need to find the courage to let them go. We will be
taking a much more healthy approach to the nature of the
faith journey if we do. The young person may still want to
meet with us on occasion, but the nature of the relationship
again has to change. We must reassure them that we are not
rejecting them: it is simply that we have travelled with them
as far as we can. Now it is time for them to move on without
us, in someone else's company. While we will continue to
pray for them, and offer encouragement and support, they

must make a new start in order to make new discoveries.

The end of one journey is the beginning of another

When the road parts for us as fellow travellers on the journey of faith, we bid our farewell and watch as they meet other travellers and forge ahead without us. But here is an opportunity for us to look around and see if there is someone else who needs our company as they travel along the Way. Accompanying young people is not a one-time commitment but something we should commit ourselves to over and over again. At every parting of the ways, it is more than likely that there will be another young person looking for company on the road ahead, needing someone to lean on.

A summary in sound bites

- Be prepared for the time when you will have to say goodbye.

- Don't hold on for longer than you are meant to.

- Amidst change, rethink how you can best accompany your companion.

- Let your companion go when the time comes for them to travel on with someone else.

- Encourage your fellow traveller to make new companions.

- Keep your parting promises.

- It is a long road, with many travellers. Take the opportunity to draw alongside new companions yourself.

- Treasure the memories.

Chapter 10

A WORD TO PARENTS AND CHURCH LEADERS

What life have you if you have not life together?
There is no life that is not in community,
And no community not lived in praise of God.

T S Eliot, Choruses from *The Rock*, 1934

In my experience of over ten years of youth ministry I have had to recognise that both church leaders and parents have a significant influence on young people's faith development. Parents who are part of a faith community will often exert a great deal of pressure on their children to conform to the demands of church life. While this may be acceptable when they are children, as young people move into early adulthood this pressure can become a critical stumbling block to faith. Church leaders grow concerned at the number of teenagers who abandon the church, and will often jump on the latest youth trend in their desire to hang on to their remaining youth. Youth leaders come under pressure to do more and to do it effectively. The whole experience of youth and church can become quite messy, with casualties on both sides.

Despite all our efforts, across the UK hundreds of young people still leave our churches every single week. Thousands of young people find themselves either abandoned by the faith community or remove themselves from it. And hundreds of thousands of young people are crying out for meaningful relationships as they progress along the journey of life, a journey that is all the richer when it becomes a journey of faith. The following letters are my plea to parents and to the church to take relationships between adults and young people more seriously.

Dear parents

How precious your children are to you. You have cared for and nurtured them since they first saw the light of day. In their first few months you spent sleepless nights as they adjusted to life outside the comfort of the womb. You saw their first smile and nursed them through their first illness. You remember when they first crawled and walked, the first time they said 'Mama' or 'Dada'. You watched them play and make their first friends. You watched as they learnt about the world, and sought to keep them from danger. You sang them to sleep at night, praying that God would protect them. You nervously saw them depart for their first day at school. You watched them compete, standing on the sidelines and cheering your lungs out even when they came in last. You took them along to church and Sunday school in the hope that they would learn good moral values and have a share in your faith. How innocent their prayers seemed as they asked God for such simple things. You remember the birthdays and the Christmases, and the fun you had together.

How could they grow up? Only yesterday you were bathing them and changing their nappies. Only yesterday they needed you. But they are older now. How big and scary their first day at secondary school seemed. You remember their first school report and how worried you were that they might not succeed. You remember them in deep distress because of bullying, how you were angry and wanted to see justice done. You remember the first time they stayed away from home without you, the first night they came in late, driving you mad with worry. You remember the first time they lied to you because they wanted to do what their friends did and knew you wouldn't approve.

This is your precious child. You have worked long and

hard to give them all they needed so that they might grow up strong and wise. The time has come to let them venture out on their own. They want to grow up. They want to do, hear, feel and see things for themselves. They need the space to find faith for themselves; they can't depend on your faith any longer. You cannot run this race for them; but even if they fail, you must still be there cheering your lungs out as they cross the line. Now is an important time, and there are no easy formulas. You cannot be sure what decision they will make. They may not always want your advice. They want to enter the adult world, to make their own choices and accept responsibility. It won't happen all at once, it can't happen all at once, but it will happen. And it is better that it happens while you are there to encourage and support them, to pick them up when they fall, to tell them they are loved when someone breaks their heart.

But they need other adults to support them too: then, should they stumble, if they cannot or will not turn to you, they still have someone to lean on. So let them form strong friendships with adults you can trust. Pray that God will draw faithful Christians alongside them. You are key to allowing this to happen. It won't be easy, and at times you may feel as though you are being pushed out of their life. But for your child's sake, so that they might have a long and richly blessed journey of faith, you must try.

From a fellow traveller in Christ,
Paul.

Dear church leaders

I can see your concern that young people are leaving the church and abandoning their faith. The consequences are painful and worrying. It spells despair for many ageing congregations who have no one to pass on the baton of faith to. It leaves a cultural vacuum in the church. You look to yourselves and ask, 'What can we do?'

You have run youth fellowships and youth groups; you have organised Sunday schools and after-church activities, and allowed groups to run youth services and all sorts of weird and wonderful things. You have subsidised youth weekends and trips to youth festivals. You have stood up on Sunday mornings and announced the great need for more youth leaders and people to work with the youth. You have done everything you can think of to try to persuade the young people to stick with the church. You want them to understand all you have done for them, how you long for them to mature in the faith. You have prayed and laboured, but the number of young people within your church has gone on dwindling and declining. What more can you do?

Is it possible the church has made a mistake? Did all those youth activities really bring young people into contact with the real heart of the church? Though they had some good times with each other, did you provide the young with opportunities to be part of the whole congregation? Or did you end up distancing them from the wider church, leaving them with no real sense of belonging? And have you encouraged responsible adults within your faith community to draw close and form relationships with young people? Or did you think that appointing a youth worker would be enough? How well do you, personally, know the young people in your church? Is there even one young person you know well, or have you too put a distance between 'us and them'?

Young people need to know they can trust the rest of the faith community and be accepted by them. They need to be able to contribute alongside adults, not simply from within the youth ghetto we have created. They need opportunities to build strong relationships with adults and the support of the church leadership to do this. Could you make the time to invest in a young person's life? Perhaps then they will begin to feel that they belong to the faith community. Perhaps then we will see them turn to the church and say, 'These people care. They are interested in me, in seeing me grow. They want me to be a part of who they are. They have a real and an honest faith. They believe in God, and he is real to them. He makes a difference to their lives.' Perhaps one day it will no longer be 'us and them', but simply *us*?

Adults have so much to offer young people, and young people have so much to offer adults. Can we work together on this? Can we all move forward on a journey of faith in the same Lord Jesus Christ, who we all follow and long to know more nearly and more dearly? Please walk with young people on this journey, travelling alongside as their companions, sharing in their stories and letting them share in yours. Let God make of them what he will. Let them learn from your experience of what God has done with you. But don't be disappointed if they choose not to follow in your footsteps. Encourage them to find their own path in God. And don't hold so tightly to your traditions that it prevents you from looking forward to the riches God longs to give us all as we faithfully serve him. My prayer is that we will finish this journey together.

Your brother in Christ,

Paul.

Epilogue

BON VOYAGE!

There are two words used a great deal by Jesus in the Gospels. One is 'come' and the other is 'go'. It is no use coming unless you go, and it is no use going unless you come.

It would be a week they would never forget. The two friends had celebrated with tremendous joy and yet experienced a depth of sadness they had never known before. The events of the previous week troubled them. It was time to return home. They decided to walk back to their small village seven miles away. It was a long and lonely walk, but they had things to say and needed the time to talk through what had happened.

They had not travelled far when they noticed another figure following some distance behind them. Eventually the man drew alongside. Happening to overhear their conversation, he remarked, 'You seem to be in deep discussion about something.'

The two friends were too weary to tell him to mind his own business. But, after a brief pause, he spoke again: 'What are you so concerned about?'

The two stopped dead in their tracks and glared at the stranger. Cleopas snapped, 'Don't you know what's been happening over the past few days? Where have you been? On the moon?'

The traveller had a gleam of light in his eyes as he asked,

'What's been happening then?'

The two shook their heads and they started to walk once more. Cleopas explained the events of the week that had just passed. How their hopes had been raised and then crushed. How there had been celebration and dancing, betrayal and intrigue, tragedy and forgiveness, ambition and mystery.

When he had finished there was a long silence as they tramped along. Then the stranger spoke. What he said was compelling, enlightening and full of wisdom. They hung onto every word until they reached their small village.

At this point their fellow traveller made as if he was going to continue his journey, but Cleopas urged him to stay and eat with them. He accepted their invitation.

They had sat down at the table to eat, and Cleopas invited the stranger to say the prayer of blessing. He picked up a small loaf of bread and asked God to bless it. Then he broke it and handed a piece to each of them. Suddenly it dawned on them who he was. Jesus! Alive! It had been his voice they had heard, his wisdom they had received as they had walked along the road to Emmaus. They rubbed their eyes and gasped with astonishment. But while they were still gathering their wits about them, they realised that he was no longer there. He had vanished.

The journey begins when we go

This story from Luke 24:13–35 is a powerful description of how Jesus met two of his followers after his resurrection. It also contains other insights as we consider the nature of our faith as a journey. The story itself is, in essence, what this book is all about. Two travelling companions begin a journey together. Along the way they engage in deep discussion about their beliefs, and struggle with the doubts and questions that have been forced on them by circumstance. They have experienced much together; they have seen great changes take place; they have celebrated; they have been in the wilderness.

As their journey progresses they discover that they have a new companion, Jesus (though they don't recognise him at first). He challenges them; they ask questions; he responds; they grow in knowledge. Suddenly they realise who he is, and this recognition brings about profound change. They finally understand the truth. A revolution in their faith has taken place. They have moved closer to Christ through having experienced the journey with him.

If we want to meet with God, then we must take our place alongside fellow travellers on the journey of faith. To do this we must take Jesus' commission seriously (Matt 28:19–20) and be on the look out for people we can make the journey with. I pray you will take up this challenge and respond by choosing to be in a place where you can form relationships with young people and set off on the journey with them. I pray that it will be a rich and fruitful time for you both. Some of what you have read here will help you. But, like the two disciples on the road to Emmaus, you do not travel alone. Jesus will walk with you, even though you will not always recognise him. He will never leave you. He will be the one you can lean on when the going gets tough and you are overcome by despair. He is the constant companion, and he never tires of accompanying us.

And so, farewell

Goodbye always seems so final to me. I've never been very good at saying it. I prefer to slip away so that I leave unnoticed, without fuss. Then I am left with the fond memories and hope in what's to come. But, though in life we may experience many goodbyes, on the journey of faith we have a firm grasp on hope for the future. With Jesus and our fellow travellers beside us, encouraging us to press on, we can keep going till the end of the race, when all things will be made complete and our journey finally comes to an end. Perhaps this book has been a helpful guide to you along the

Appendix 1

Suggestions for secure relationships

In the light of considerable media attention regarding child abuse, we must respond to protect children from potential abuse situations. All churches and youth organisations are encouraged to adopt a child protection policy, and you should enquire whether your church has one. If so, then it is important that this is respected. If it has not, the church would be wise to adopt one.

There is a national advisory service which offers excellent advice and training for churches wishing to adopt a policy. They can be contacted at the address below: **The Churches' Child Protection Advisory Service (CCPAS), PO Box 133, Swanley, Kent, BR8 7UQ; tel 01322 667207, fax 01322 614788**. The CCPAS can also be contacted for advice if a young person discloses any information about abuse to you.

It is also important to consider your own safety and potential situations where you could be accused of abuse. It is important to point out that this is extremely rare, but we would be wise to consider possibilities in advance. I have suggested five simple precautions below, but these are by no means exhaustive. Again, I suggest you refer to the child protection policy in your own church or youth organisations for further advice.

- Before you start meeting with young people, let your church leaders know what you are doing. Make contact with the young people's parents to let them know too.

- Always make sure someone knows where you are going and who will be with you, whether this is a church leader, parents or a friend.

- Try not to meet with a young person on your own behind locked doors, where others do not have easy access or where you are not visible.

- Be open about what you do when you meet with young people. This will help to remove the suspicion that some people have about adults who mix with young people. It also helps other adults to see relationships with young people as natural and not 'odd'. It may even encourage them to get involved themselves.

- Most importantly, don't be afraid of forming natural and expressive relationships with young people because of child protection issues. They are there to protect, not prevent. We should not allow those who abuse the young to spoil what should be healthy and valuable relationships. If we do, then we ignore the needs of the young and are ourselves guilty of a different form of abuse – neglect.

Appendix 2

Christian organisations involved in global aid projects

Christian Aid, 35 Lower Marsh, Waterloo, London, SE1 7RT; tel (0171) 620 4444. www.christian-aid.org.uk

Works in over 60 countries, helping people, regardless of religion or race, to improve their lives and tackle the causes of poverty and injustice.

Oasis Trust, 115 Southwark Bridge Road, London, SE1 0AX; tel (0171) 450 9000. www.u-net.com/oasis/

Provides hostels for the homeless, fair-trade employment and projects that counter poverty and injustice around the world.

Tear Fund, 100 Church Road, Teddington, Middx, TW11 8QE; tel (0181) 977 9144. www.tear fund.org.uk

An international relief organisation and promoter of fair trade, providing resources to be used in churches, with specific youth resources and programmes on offer.

World Vision, 599 Avebury Boulevard, Milton Keynes, MK9 3PG; tel (01908) 841000. www.24hourfamine.org.uk

Helps to relieve world poverty in crisis situations and through long-term projects, and offers opportunities to sponsor children in the developing world. You can take part in the national 24-Hour Famine project to raise funds for their work. Packs available from the address above.

Appendix 3

Organisations offering outreach opportunities for young people

Oasis Trust (see Appendix 2) operates Frontline Teams involved in outreach and support for projects at home and abroad. Also on offer are short- and long-term placements with a range of possible projects, from urban safe-houses to working in slums in South America.

Scripture Union, 207–209 Queensway, Bletchley, Milton Keynes, MK2 2EB; tel (01908) 856000. www.scripture.org.uk
  Offers outreach opportunities through short-term missions and holidays in England and Wales, as well as long-term projects at home and abroad.

Youth for Christ, PO Box 5254, Halesowen, West Midlands, B63 3DG; tel (0121) 550 8055. www.yfc.co.uk
  Operates several short- and long-term outreach projects in the UK, including Street Invaders, Operation Gideon and Activate.

Youth with a Mission (YWAM), Highfield Oval, Harpenden, Herts, AL5 4BX; tel (01582) 463300. www.ywam-england.com
  Offers several outreach projects and training courses for young people, at home and abroad.

Appendix 4

Holiday opportunities for young people

Covies, 11–13 Lower Hillgate, Stockport, SK1 1JQ; tel (0161) 474 1262. http://dialspace.dial.pipex.com/town/avenue/vr30/
Offers a range of summer holidays for young people. Brochures available from the address above.

Crusaders, 2 Romeland Hill, St Albans, Herts, AL3 4ET; tel (01727) 855422. www.crusaders.org.uk
Offers a range of summer holidays for young people. Brochures available from the address above.

Greenbelt, The Greenhouse, St Luke's Church, Hillmarton Road, London, N7 9JE; tel (0171) 700 6585. www.greenbelt.org.uk
The annual festival run over the August bank holiday weekend.

Scripture Union (see Appendix 3) offers a range of holidays around the year for young people, including Countdown. Brochures available from the address above.

Spring Harvest, 14 Horsted Square, Uckfield, East Sussex, TN22 1QL; tel (01825) 769111. www.springh.org.uk
An annual event run over Easter, which caters for the whole church, with an extensive youth programme.

Soul Survivor, 37 Quickly Lane, Chorleywood, Herts, WD3 5AE; tel (01923) 446655.
Runs two major summer festivals and smaller weekend activities.

Appendix 5

Further reading

Andy Hickford, *Essential Youth*, Kingsway (0 85476 661 8): challenges the church to listen to teenagers in order to be effective in mission.

Stephen D Jones, *Faith Shaping*, Judson Press (0 8170 1118 8): comprehensive but readable book about adolescence and the experience of faith. Written out of the author's experience of youth ministry in the USA.

Kevin Ford, *Jesus for a New Generation*, Hodder & Stoughton (0 0340 66911 X): in-depth look at understanding and reaching Generation X within an American context.

Gunter Krallmann, *Mentoring for Mission*, Globe Europe (9627 415057): theological background to mentoring, apprenticeship and discipleship.

John Buckeridge (ed), *Nurturing Young Disciples*, Marshall Pickering (0 551 02948 X): broad study of the issues surrounding discipling young people, with chapters by Paul Borthwick, Tony Campolo, Duffy Robbins, John Allan and Kathy Holkeboer.

Nick Pollard, *Why Do They Do That?*, Lion (0 7459 37608): explores the reasons why teenagers do the things they do.

Pete Ward, *Youthwork and the Mission of God*: Frameworks for relational outreach, SPCK (0 281 05044 9): explores the 'how to' behind outreach to young people, with an emphasis on what it means to be relational.

Available from Scripture Union

Serious Prayer
Trev Gregory
1 85999 095 9, £5.99
Lively and practical, this book helps youth leaders communicate to their groups the importance and relevance of prayer. 'The approach taken is superb' *(Youthwork magazine)*. Ideal for use with the *Serious Prayer* video.

Serious Prayer video
1 85999 099 1, £14.99
Five fast-moving and motivating programmes aimed at 15-19 year olds, presenting the basic whys, whats and hows of serious prayer. A challenging approach with the strong central theme that prayer not only changes situations but also changes us and our relationship with God. 'This is a great resource in its own right' *(Youthwork magazine)*.

Young People and Small Groups
Danny Brierley
1 85999 211 0, £5.99
A ministry based on small groups can give young people a greater sense of belonging and achievement. This excellent resource will help church-based youth workers who are looking to engender deeper growth in the lives of the young people they are responsible for.

Disclosure: Go one on one with God
A5 booklet, £2.50
A radically different Bible reading guide for young people. Published bi-monthly, these notes are produced in a style that will appeal to the 15+ age group. With readings for every weekday and special articles on relevant issues, group discussion starters, suggestions for further reading, music, film and TV reviews

Making It Work
Stephen Gaukroger
0 86201 632 0, £3.99
Explores how to take the first vital steps towards having an effective Christian life. Includes an Action Guide for small groups, to help put the ideas outlined into practice.

Oh No, Not the Nativity! Sketches through the church year
1 85999 233 1, £6.99
More than twenty new sketches for use in church services, written for festivals and special events all year round. Suitable for all levels of experience and appealing to all ages, with a variety of styles and approaches. A photocopiable resource.

Scrap Happy
Joan King with Footprints Theatre Company
1 85999 014 2, £7.99
A five-session resource for people of all ages, designed to build cross-generational friendships. the programme centres around the Scrap Family and is designed to be used with *Scrap Happy: The Video* (**1 85999 143 2, £14.99**). A photocopiable resource.

Undrugged and Still Dancing: The facts on drugs and alcohol
Debbie Goddard
1 85999 177 7, £4.99
Using true-life stories to help us understand, this book presents the facts on drugs and alcohol, explains what the risks are and shows what we can do to help when people we know get involved.

Make Me a Channel
Roy Lawrence
1 85999 015 0, £4.99
This book highlights the struggle many Christians have in achieving the balance between receiving from God and giving to others. Without God's input, our good intentions flounder; but if we don't share his gifts, we are not being the people he wants us to be.

How to Pray When Life Hurts
Roy Lawrence
0 86201 240 6, £6.99
Prayer makes a difference because God makes a difference. Whether we feel guilty or angry, fearful or under pressure, this book offers practical help on how to pray when life hurts.

All these products are available from your local Christian bookshop, or from **SU Mail Order, PO Box 764, Oxford, OX4 5FJ; tel (01865) 716880, fax (01865) 715152**. Please add £0.75 postage and packaging for the first book, and £0.50 for subsequent books, up to a maximum of £2.75.

For a complete catalogue of resources from Scripture Union, please contact **SU Sales and Promotions, 207-209 Queensway, Bletchley, Milton Keynes, MK2 2EB; tel (01908) 856000, fax (01908) 856111**.